DIS-ORDERED

*A Christian Journey Through the
Problem of Evil & Suffering*

Paul Anleitner

Goodmakers

ISBN-13: 9798218042950

Cover design by: Mitchell McCleary
Library of Congress Control Number: 2018675309
Printed in the United States of America

To my wife, Keri-

There is no conceivable way that I could have come to this point in my journey with God without you as my deepest, closest companion journeying together with me. For every shared moment of joy, grief, question, or wonder, I give thanks to have been tangled up in it all with you. I love you.

CONTENTS

WHERE ARE YOU, GOD?

It was early in the month of March. The year was 2020. I'll never forget the moment my wife pulled me into the hallway just outside of our bedroom, "There have been cases happening in Minnesota. At what point do you think we need to start getting concerned for Justice?" Justice, our oldest son, has a history of severe asthma. It used to be that even the slightest common cold could end in an ambulance trip to the ICU for him. With a novel, highly contagious virus that seemed to attack the lungs spreading throughout China and Italy at unprecedented rates, a growing sense of "this might happen here..." began to brew even in our safe, insular Midwest.

Initially (and in hindsight, foolishly), I dismissed her concern. We don't live during the Middle Ages. Plagues don't happen here in the U.S. Only a couple of weeks later, I got home late from a meeting at church and found my wife unusually glued to the television set. "Tom Hanks has the coronavirus...so does an NBA player...and now they are canceling the rest of NBA games!" At that moment, I felt as if reality had shifted into the Twilight Zone. Not long after that, we were canceling our church services, locking down entire states, and braving the grocery store with masks and work gloves on to protect ourselves from this mysterious plague.

Over two years later (as of the date of the writing of this introduction), more than one million Americans have died because of COVID 19. It's a staggering number that seems far beyond any ability to emotionally quantify. Yet, as heartbreaking as this is, it isn't the only suffering people have endured during the pandemic. People lost businesses. They lost out on important milestones and life moments like a high school graduation or wedding. They lost the dignity of even being able to hold a public funeral for a friend or loved one. Incidents of self-harm, suicide, and abuse skyrocketed. Families and churches have split over conspiracies and the politicization of the pandemic.

> We have all suffered.
> We have all had our faith tested.
> We have all asked,
> *"Where are you, God?"*

I remember the first time I asked this question. I was just a boy. In my church tradition growing up, we believed that Jesus' death on the cross not only paid the price for human sin, but it also paid the price for our physical healing, and if we only had enough faith, we could access right now the perfect healing that Jesus died for. This tradition is often called the *Word of Faith* movement by those in it and the *prosperity gospel* by those outside it. So when our pastor's sister was diagnosed with cancer, each of us in the church threw all the faith we had into trying to claim that healing for her. I remember going to prayer meetings as a kid where we had a script of "faith confessions" to speak out over her to tap into that reservoir of healing power we all believed we had "legal" spiritual access to as believers in Jesus.

As a boy, this made some degree of sense, and the incredible stories of healing claimed by TV faith televangelists like Benny Hinn and Oral Roberts only bolstered the credibility of our beliefs. If this strategy worked for Benny Hinn, why not for us? The problem was that it started to seem like our faith wasn't enough. Her condition steadily worsened.

While the medical attention in the hospital intensified, our family started having her son come and stay with us. One day, my mom and dad pulled me and my younger siblings aside and told us that the boy's mom had just died and that his dad was coming to our house to pick him up and deliver the news that no boy should ever have to hear. I remember sitting on the living room couch in our small, one-story house in our blue-collar suburb on the edge of Detroit. The sofa couldn't have been more than three steps from the front door. The boy's father, who stood at least 6'4, carried an immeasurable sorrow on his face. He took his son by the hand and led him about five steps across the living room and into the shared bedroom of my brother and me to tell the young boy what no father should have to tell his son. They closed the door, and I sat there on the couch and waited.

"*Where are you, God?*"

I don't remember how long they were in there, but I don't recall it being a long time. It was quiet. No sorrowful wailing. Just silence. When they emerged, I don't remember seeing tears on their faces. Maybe there was, but all I remember was the quiet. They walked towards the door; the father said something to my parents, then they got in their cars and drove home.

The experience didn't devastate my young faith, but in the following weeks, I remember the question shifting from, "where are you, God?" to "where were you, God?" Sometimes I would listen to the conversations the adults in our church quietly had after service about their own "*where were you, God?*" questions. The theological framework of our particular tradition didn't leave them with many options other than different variations of, "Maybe she really didn't have enough faith to be healed?" I even heard some adults talk about the book of Job and how what happened to Job was because Job had secret fears... and if you're in fear, then you can't be *in* faith. That idea seemed terrifying. How can I not be afraid if my secret fears might bring about Job-like suffering? Now I'm afraid of my fears!

As I got into my early adult years, a string of suffering-inducing events pushed me to reassess the faith I had received.

From my vantage point, the faith I had received was the Christian faith. We were proudly "full-Gospel" (as opposed to those Baptists down the street, who must have only had 50% of the Gospel), and we were "Spirit-filled." We had the real thing, and everyone else had man-made religious traditions that polluted the truth of the Bible. Now, at this point, some of you may be saying aloud, "You thought you had the real Christian faith?! You guys were a prosperity gospel church!!" Yet I suspect many of you possibly had the same dispositions towards other Christian denominations and theological traditions outside of your tribe.

There are various problems with this kind of attitude, but one of the practical ways this sort of ecclesiology becomes particularly problematic is when you brush up against profound questions that you feel have not been answered well in your church or denomination. This leaves you feeling as if you've exhausted the well of resources available to followers of Jesus. When the tradition you've inhabited appears to you to be the definitive standard of what Christianity is and your theology can't adequately address the questions you're grappling with, it is not abnormal to feel like you have to leave the Christian story and Christian community for better answers.

But I don't think you do. Maybe like a younger version of me, you just need to discover a broader Christian perspective. Perhaps you need to see that there could be some blind spots or even some flat-out hurtful theological ideas in the version of the Christian story you've received. You need not throw out every good thing you've received from your theological tradition in order to open yourself up to the breadth and depth of available resources in the historic, global Christian tradition.

We need every available resource at our disposal when it comes to grappling with questions about evil and suffering, because few things call into question the story we believe about God, the world, and our place in it all, quite like an experience of unexplained suffering or evil. Certainly, there's a nearly endless catalog of Christian books on the problem of evil ranging from easy-to-read "how to" manuals from pastors or popular Christian authors on what we should do when we're suffering or facing evil to dense philosophical treatises that attempt to address every possible metaphysical minutia that relates to God's will, evil, or suffering. This book inhabits the liminal space between those two approaches to offer you:

1) An overview of relevant biblical literature on evil and suffering

2) An impartial tour through Christian history to explore how some of the most important Christian thinkers from across the theological spectrum attempted to address the problem of evil

3) What I hope will be, by the time we've reached our conclusion, an intellectually and existentially satisfying response to some of our deepest questions about evil and suffering built from the biblical literature and synthesized from some of the great Christian minds of the past

While questions that we may only dare to whisper in our moments of profound confusion or sorrow may be the most existentially pressing questions in that moment, it's not hard for us to tug on the thread of that set of questions and slowly find out that this thread is woven into a much larger and more connected fabric of challenging faith questions.

-Is all suffering evil?

- If God knows the outcome, why pray at all?

-Why does it seem like Jesus heals everyone but in the Old Testament, it seems like God smites people for all sorts of reasons?

-Can we really blame all of the world's suffering on Adam and Eve's sin?

-Is this really the best world God could have made? Did He not want to make a better world, or maybe He couldn't for some reason? Couldn't He have made one without plagues, world wars, and Holocausts?

I list these questions not as some exhaustive list that we'll systematically go through and answer line by line but merely to illustrate that the immediate questions that often emerge out of our own particular run-in with an instance of evil or suffering often lead us to ask all sorts of questions that are theologically and philosophically related.

A word about how I have constructed this book and my convictional location that I think is relevant before you embark on the first chapter- we will begin in Part I by exploring some of the relevant biblical literature surrounding questions of evil, suffering, and God's will. Realizing some of the challenges to interpretation, especially as one compares Old Testament and New Testament texts, we will begin in Part II & III to work our way through the perspectives of important Christians from the past and see how they have attempted to make sense of the biblical data and their experiences of evil and suffering. As a fact of history, the writings of Christian men have played an overwhelmingly disproportionate role in shaping Christian theology until relatively recently. My admission of women from the past is not due to intentional bias; instead, it is due to the simple fact that it has been the Augustine's, Aquinas', Luther's, and Calvin's of history that have, for better or worse, had the most profound impact on the way both Christian men and women think about God, evil, and suffering.

I have not intended to write this book as an apologetic or sales pitch for any particular denomination or tradition. I have a convictional location that I interpret the world and the Bible from (we all do!); but for the first fifteen chapters of this book, my goal will be to act to the best of my abilities as an impartial tour guide through the biblical literature and the history of

Christian thought on the problem of evil so that you can have your perspective broadened too. Whether you are a seminary grad who's familiar with names like Origen or Thomas Aquinas, or if just you're a hungry learner with no formal academic training but a lot of questions about God, evil, and suffering, I'm confident this book will help you discover valuable insights and consider divergent perspectives on the problem of evil that you hadn't considered before.

In Part IV, I will shift from being an impartial tour guide to sharing my conclusions with you. I offer my *theodicy*, meaning how I address the problem of evil and suffering, not to say, "it's my way or the highway, pal!" but to humbly offer it for your consideration as someone who has wrestled with this subject personally and professionally for decades. My own experience is that going on the guided tour that I will lead you on in this book has changed the way I think and given me better answers to some of my deepest questions. I also present my theodicy conclusions to show *how* I have attempted to find answers to some of my deepest questions through a better understanding of Scripture and by synthesizing some of the best theological and philosophical resources in our broad, historic Christian tradition.

I want to bless you to disagree with my conclusions or the conclusions of any of the far greater minds of the past that I will highlight in the pages of this book. Simultaneously, I want to encourage you to comb through these pages with a spirit of openness and intellectual curiosity. Based on your own unique church experience (or lack thereof), you will likely enter into this book with some biases towards or against certain theological voices mentioned within these pages. That's okay. My hope as your tour guide is to offer you both their most convincing arguments and some of the strongest objections against their perspectives so that you could thoughtfully evaluate both sides.

I want to thank the listeners of my podcast *Deep Talks: Exploring Theology & Meaning-Making* for provoking me with so many profound questions about God, evil, and suffering over the years. Your questions challenged me to systematically comb through two-thousand years of Christian theological history so that I could faithfully present a wide range of options from our broad Christian tradition for addressing these profound questions. Your enthusiasm and encouragement about the work I did on this subject for that podcast series birthed in me a desire to offer this book as a culmination of that intellectual and spiritual journey. It is my hope that this work not only provides an intellectually satisfying journey through your most difficult questions about God, evil, and suffering but that this would be a road map to navigate, in the very existence of your daily lives, the experiences of suffering you encounter in the world.

Finally, though I have not intended this book to be specifically for professional academics, I have included endnotes so that you can do the diligent follow-up work of not only checking my sources but continuing on your journey to read the important works of others on this subject. I am especially indebted to the work of Charlene Burns and her *Christian Understandings of Evil: The Historical Trajectory* for being the first proper academic book I had ever stumbled across to offer a historical survey on theological responses to the problem of evil. Her painstaking scholarship to comb through an unfathomable number of primary sources and catalog quotations and citations inspired me to launch the original podcast series, and now this book, in a similar fashion. I could not have done this without her groundbreaking work first.

PART I - OUR QUESTIONS & THE BIBLE

1. WHAT MAKES THE PROBLEM OF EVIL A PROBLEM?

Several years ago, I found myself sharing in a moment of anguished prayer with a couple who had just lost their child. I will never forget the cries of grief that poured out of the mother that day, nor will I forget the funeral in the week that followed. Caskets should not be built that small. This wasn't the first time I had seen a tiny casket, but that never makes it any easier. Though every death brings with it an experience of grief, some deaths feel more explainable than others. I don't find myself overcome by questions when the lifelong chain-smoker comes down with lung cancer and dies. I feel grief, but I don't have as many questions about causality.

Sitting at this funeral, I felt that old haunting question well up within my soul- *"where are you, God?"* It is the question I asked when the boy I mentioned in the introduction lost his mother. It is the question I asked when I watched the World Trade Center Towers collapse on live television in 2001. It is the question I asked when a tsunami devastated southeast Asia just a few years later, killing hundreds of thousands. It is the question I asked the first time I spent a few nights in the ICU at the children's hospital with my son and saw bald children from chemotherapy treatments living in the hospital as if it were their home. It is a question we all likely asked as the world descended into uncertainty and chaos in 2020 as the coronavirus spread. Questions about God, evil, and suffering have not only perplexed even the most committed Christians, causing many to abandon their faith, but these questions also act as some of the most significant barriers to faith for the atheist and earnest spiritual seeker alike.

Questions about the problem of evil are no mere abstract, philosophical conundrum relegated to a university lecture hall or an academic theological journal. No, the questions that emerge in our experiences of tragic loss and suffering are the tangible, lived questions of theology and philosophy that strike us at the very core of our being and threaten our sense of meaning and purpose in the world. Though these discussions sometimes descend into a seemingly distant realm of philosophical abstraction, we mustn't be afraid of theology or philosophy if we are going to address these questions well. Whether we are aware of it or not, these disciplines are foundational to our efforts to find meaning in the world. Because of this, we will want to work through them thoughtfully and with intellectual curiosity.

As a somewhat silly illustration of this point, try this fun experiment sometime. Remember that old party game some people called "Six Degrees of Kevin Bacon" where you had to think of a seemingly unrelated celebrity and trace their relational connections back to the actor, Kevin Bacon? What you surprisingly uncovered in that game was that most anyone you could think of was only six relational steps away from knowing Kevin Bacon. As innocuous and asinine as that game seemed, it opened you up to seeing how relationally connected we all are to others we thought we shared nothing in common with. Well, there's a fun little variation of that kind of game that can help you see how necessary a discipline like philosophy truly is.

Look up a random word on Wikipedia. Click the first available link in the description that isn't a pronunciation-related link. Then wherever that link takes you, do the same thing again with that word. Repeat enough times, and you will eventually get to *philosophy*. I like basketball, so I did this experiment by starting with a Wikipedia search for "LeBron James." I mean, there's no way NBA superstar LeBron James has any relevant connection to philosophy, right? I got to philosophy in six clicks! So don't be afraid of philosophy or theology; LeBron James depends on it!

You and I are not alone in our questions. Even if your particular church experience has made you feel like hard questions aren't welcome, I can tell you that Christians, throughout the ages, have wrestled with just about every question that could enter your mind. There are endless volumes of written evidence out there to prove it too. I bring that up not only as some sort of consolation or as a license to ask questions for those who've simply never been given permission, but also as an encouragement to not deal with your profound questions alone on some solitary, internal island of your thoughts. My encouragement to you instead is to try and exhaust every available resource that Christians past and present have produced to find better solutions to the questions that perplex you, and do it in a community with others. I hope that this book can be one of those resources.

Obviously, it is not just Christians who wrestle with questions about God, evil, and suffering. However, for the purposes of this book, we're going to primarily focus on how differing Christians have responded to the problem of evil. In fact, a Greek philosopher living approximately 300 years before Christ's birth named Epicurus may have best presented the fundamental question about God, evil, and suffering when he asked:

> "Is God willing to prevent evil, but not able? Then he is not omnipotent. Is he able, but not willing? Then he is malevolent. Is he both able and willing? Then whence cometh evil? Is he neither able nor willing?
>
> Then why call him God?" [1]

Though we may lack the rhetorical skills of an Epicurus

necessary to distill all of our questions about God, evil, and suffering down to such a succinct and profound summarization, doesn't this provocation from Epicurus truly get at the heart of all our questions about evil and suffering? After all, if God is truly all-powerful, He could just decide to eradicate the coronavirus, cancer, war, and famine right now at this very moment, couldn't He? If one answers, "Yes, of course!" You're left with the uncomfortable counterpoint of, "Well, why hasn't He stopped every instance of suffering or evil in creation then?" Does that mean that He's just not willing to? If one responds, "No! Of course, He doesn't want terrible things to happen! God is good, and He never wills for evil..." then the question circles back around to, "So if He doesn't want evil to happen, but evil happens, aren't you saying He just *can't* do anything to stop it?"

Of course, entangled within those questions are other layers of questions about the purpose of prayer, God's love and power, Satan and spiritual beings, free will and predestination... on and on the questions go! Some people may prefer to quietly stuff these questions away deep in some closet space in their mind, while others may become so discouraged by their questions (and often the unhelpful answers the people in their lives have given them) that they just throw in the towel on God altogether.

I don't believe either one of these responses are helpful. Eventually, that dark closet in your mind will get too full, and all the questions will spill out. Grief often has a funny way of doing that to us. Leaving the Christian story for some other religious tradition isn't going to make these questions go away either. Considering leaving the Christian story to become, say, a Muslim to get away from these questions? Sorry. They are wrestling with the problem of evil too. What about Buddhism? Good luck. Now I think the Buddha had a decent bit of practical wisdom to share, but when the Buddha teaches that behind it all is *śūnyatā* or emptiness, I don't find that to be a more compelling or helpful answer. Maybe just throw it all out and become a Rick Sanchez-styled selfish nihilist (or Tyler Durden for the old Millenials and

Gen X'ers)? They might make for some dark and twisted on-screen laughs (even that point is debatable), but no one wants to be around those people in real life.

As I regularly counsel people considering leaving the Christian story and Christian community because of their unanswered questions- you should make sure you get to know what you are leaving first before you go. Your particular church experience and theological tradition is just a tiny part of the larger whole of Christianity. It may even be a distorted view at that. Don't confuse your particular church experience with all that the Christian story and Christian community has to offer. There's more to explore.

Any effort to try and address these questions and formulate a response is doing what theologians and philosophers often call *theodicy*. The term theodicy comes from a 17th-18th century mathematician, theologian and philosopher named Gottfried Leibniz (who we will explore more in chapter 11). Leibniz constructed the word *theodicy* by using the Greek prefix *theo* meaning "God" and the suffix *dike* meaning "justice" to create a term that describes philosophical or theological efforts to defend God's goodness and justice in the face of evil and suffering. These days theodicy can broadly refer to anything having to do with the problem of evil.

For better or worse, there hasn't been a singular, univocal response in Christianity to the problem of evil - no one theodicy to rule them all. What makes it even harder is that when we open our Bible to look for a biblical theodicy, we find what sometimes seems like conflicting answers to our questions. For example, there are no direct mentions of demons anywhere in the Old Testament, but then as we jump into the New Testament, we find Jesus performing exorcisms all over the Gospels.[2]

With that in mind, what should we do when a loved one comes down with a painful disease? Do we interpret it as something coming from God like God's curse on David's son

Absalom in 2 Samuel 12 or as some kind of evil attack of Satan like the woman who had been crippled for eighteen years in Luke 13? Is there a third "well, sometimes random bad stuff just happens" category we need to consider? Bring this question to the pastor at the local Reformed church and then go over to the pastor at the Charismatic church down the street and you'll probably get two wildly different answers. So how are you ever supposed to figure out who's right about the Bible?

A couple of tools at our disposal can help us sift through this dilemma. First, we can learn to consult vetted scholars of the Bible from a variety of traditions- scholars who do more than just give their perspectives on difficult biblical passages but show their work so you can compare and evaluate their processes. Second, we can mine the theological depths of the broad, historic, and global Christian community and compare their answers together to see if we can find any recurring threads that might shed light on some answers to our tough questions. The Apostle Paul wrote that "we all see in part" as if we're looking at a reflection in an ancient mirror - and ancient mirrors weren't as clear as the mirrors we have today. [3] Part of seeing a more complete picture on this side of glory comes by comparing what others believe to have seen as they look into the Scriptures.

To do this comparative analysis well, there is also some work that we must allow the Spirit of God to do on our hearts and minds. We cannot consult the Scriptures with our minds already made up on what the answers are to our questions. Rather, we have to humbly step into the world of the ancient author that God vested his communicative authority upon and realize that some of our questions might not even be anywhere on that inspired author's radar to address specifically. For example, we might wrestle with a question about why God would allow the dinosaurs to go extinct some 65 million years ago. If we go looking for answers about dinosaurs in Genesis, we will be horribly disappointed. The ancient author of Genesis, who is writing to an ancient near eastern people, just isn't going to have pressing questions about dinosaurs that need to be addressed. Based on the available historical evidence we have today, we can confidently say that ancient Israelites didn't even have any idea that T-rexes and stegosauruses ever existed (we'll talk more about that in chapter 13).

We don't go into a production of Shakespeare's *Macbeth* expecting there to be *Marvel* superheroes showing up in the play. We go into *Macbeth* expecting to see a rendition of the story that Shakespeare told, and we must do the same thing when we immerse ourselves into the world of the Bible. The Bible may still be for us today, but it isn't written directly to us.[4] Just like how properly attending a Shakespeare play would require that I humbly open myself up to their old English language and customs in order to understand the story correctly, I need to humbly allow the Bible to speak in its own contextual terms.

Before we begin our investigation of the biblical literature for answers, we need to establish some important terminology that will be used throughout the book. First, when working through the problem of evil, theologians and philosophers often distinguish between two kinds of evil. The first kind of evil is what we can call *moral evil*. Moral evil typically refers to the types of evil perpetrated by conscious moral agents through the misuse of their will.[5] When terrorists hijacked the planes that eventually crashed into the World Trade Center buildings on 9/11, we could more easily point to a discernible causal connection than when a small child comes down with an incurable disease. The "simplest" explanation for a horrific tragedy of moral evil like 9/11 is that human moral agents misused their free will to bring unjust suffering and death upon others. As simple as that explanation may sound, the follow-up questions about moral evils are still incredibly difficult. Why didn't God stop the hijackers? What about the husband who prayed for his wife's protection as she went off to work in downtown New York that morning, only to discover later that day that his wife died in the rubble? Why weren't his prayers answered? Why do humans even have the possibility within our "free will" to do such terrible things at all? If God didn't choose to stop that kind of evil, why should we? Explanations for why moral evils happen aren't that easy, after all.

The COVID 19 pandemic has made us all familiar with another evil, one that is usually designated as a different category from moral evils. These evils are often called *natural evils*. Natural evils are typically understood as suffering-inducing events perpetrated by "nature" and not directly by human moral agents. Though there certainly is robust debate about the possible ways human and spiritual agents (such as angels or Satan) may influence nature, most would recognize that there should still be some categorical distinction between a tsunami that kills hundreds of thousands of people and a genocidal dictator who may have accumulated a similar body count. At times, natural evils can provoke even more challenging questions about God than moral evils. Preventing an individual's moral evil, or at least knowing who to hold accountable immediately, seems like it is much more within our control than a hurricane, a pandemic, or a debilitating genetic condition.

Generally speaking, living things like to stay alive. As humans, we have an incredible array of defense mechanisms intended to keep us alive. At least some significant portion of our efforts to sort through questions about evil is driven by a desire to determine a causal pattern behind the things that could threaten our lives. Determining the causal patterns behind natural evils has not always been that easy. Science has been such a valuable discipline for helping us find the causal mechanisms that would induce natural evils. As hard as it is to believe today, there was a time when people did not understand that smoking three packs of cigarettes a day would probably give you lung cancer. We used to put leeches on the sick to drain their blood, hoping to suck the sickness out. Sometimes humans don't properly understand the difference between causation and correlation, and sometimes we just can't figure out a clear causal explanation at all.

In the absence of a clear causal explanation, what do we do? Well, historically, humans in the ancient world of the Bible were far more apt to look for "spiritual" causes for natural evils (though they wouldn't have necessarily had a categorical distinction between "material" and "spiritual" like modern Westerners do). This often led cultures to develop a pantheon of gods who controlled various elements of the natural world.

Experiencing a famine? There's a god behind that who you had better make happy quickly. Blighted with some sort of pestilence that kills your cattle? Yep, there's a god for that too. Most of Israel's neighbors, and even Israel at times, thought that the world worked just like their farming. Plant seeds, give water and sunlight, follow the right steps, and you'll get your desired crop fairly consistently. I mean, it is pretty amazing how that works...until it doesn't. What do you do then? Have you missed a step somewhere in the equation, or have you upset one of the gods?

This is the approach that most of the neighboring cultures surrounding ancient Israel took as a response to their experiences of suffering in the world, and it is within this ancient context that the Old Testament book of Job is set. If we're to use the book of Job to help us make sense of our questions about God, evil, and suffering, we will need to step into their ancient context and understand what it meant to that ancient audience first.

2. THE BOOK OF JOB: KARMA ISN'T KING

For millennia, both Jews and Christians have turned to the book of Job in times of adversity, loss, and disappointment with God. While there could be other places in the Bible where we might begin an investigation for answers about the problem of evil (certainly Genesis 2-3 would be a contender for top choice), many view the book of Job as the most direct book of theodicy in all of the Bible. It's also one of the most misunderstood books in the Bible. To better understand this book in its ancient context, we will need the help of trusted guides.

Two of my favorite guides to understanding the Old Testament are Old Testament scholars Tremper Longman III and John Walton. Both of them have given their lives to understanding the ancient Hebrew language and the cultural context of not only ancient Israel but ancient Israel's neighboring powers. Understanding the common cultural stories and myths of the ancient near eastern world is a helpful step to better understanding what is truly going on in a challenging but important book like Job. Trustworthy scholars like Longman and Walton can pick up on some of the subtle clues and "Easter eggs" embedded in the Biblical text that we might miss out on because we simply don't think like an ancient near eastern person.

For example, let's say you walked into a movie theater

without any sign out front of what was playing that day. As you sit down and the opening scene begins to play, a well-dressed couple and their young son appear on the screen. In the scene, they walk out of a theater with a sign on the marquee reading, "The Mark of Zorro." They make their way down a dark alley, and a man with a gun appears before them. What happens next? Do you know what movie you are watching? If you answered, "Oh, this is a Batman movie," how did you know that? Maybe it's because nearly every on-screen iteration of the comic book vigilante has a scene of the murder of Bruce Wayne's parents in it. As tired as many movie-goers probably are of seeing it again and again, it's a foundational narrative in Bruce Wayne/Batman's character arc.

Now, what would happen if you continued to watch the scene in this movie unfold, but instead of the armed man killing Thomas and Martha Wayne, Thomas Wayne is able to peaceably talk the would-be violent criminal out of the harm he intended and then personally offers to help rehabilitate the man and provide him gainful employment in Wayne Enterprises? That would completely change the meaning of the story. Seeing that kind of change in the movie would signal that the writer and director were trying to say something very different in this story even though they used a common cultural format with its culturally understood symbols.

Stepping into the story of Job isn't all that different from this. We just may not catch all of the relevant points of connection within that ancient culture because we're just not as familiar with those cultural stories as we are with modern superhero stories. But this is where biblical scholars can really help us. They've seen the ancient Batman movies (I'm obviously speaking analogously here, though an ancient near eastern Batman would be awesome!) and can tell us when we're watching a unique version of the Gotham City Crime Alley scene that may be getting tweaked intentionally by the author for some communicative purpose.

The book of Job isn't designed to answer all of our

questions, but there certainly is one question the book does seek to answer- "What should we think of God when disaster strikes?"[6] Israel's neighbors had their own ways of thinking about the gods when disaster struck. Most of Israel's surrounding culture believed that humanity had been made for the gods. The gods, in turn, had needs that required human attendants to take care of. These gods may need food (sacrifices), drink (libations), housing (temples), or even luxurious clothing to be brought to mediating priests because, *of course,* the gods needed to live it up. They are gods, after all.[7]

This arrangement gave human beings purpose and outlined the religious duties expected of humanity by the gods. Perform your duties well, and the gods will be good to you. Longman and Walton call this "the Great Symbiosis," but we could also borrow a term from another religious tradition that's become part of our common cultural vernacular and call this cosmic retribution principle *karma.*[8] This whole karma thing seems to work out reasonably well most of the time. In fact, even some of the other wisdom books of the Old Testament, like Proverbs, seem to celebrate the efficacy of the retribution principle or karma. Just thumb through the pages of Proverbs, and you'll see quite a few statements that seem to say, "If you do *x,* then *y* will happen." But what happens if you do *x* but instead of getting *y,* your livestock gets raided by bandits, and your children all die? This is where the wisdom of the book of Job steps in.

The key to understanding any book of the Bible is understanding the genre of the book. You don't read a comic book the same way you read an email. They have different conventions and internal rules. The book of Job follows a pretty common format and genre of writing in the Ancient Near East. We could call this "a wisdom book featuring a pious sufferer."[9] What we begin to see as we compare the book of Job with other books from the surrounding cultural context in that era (which would be around the 5th century B.C.) is that this book may borrow from a common literary genre format of its day, but the answers it gives to questions about God, evil, and suffering differ significantly from the pagan wisdom stories. [10]

We should also note that these wisdom stories featuring a pious sufferer function more like ancient thought experiments than historical biographies. Like a university philosophy professor provoking her students with a story about four people stuck at sea without enough food to feed them all or a story about a trolley car conductor who sees a group of nuns tied to one set of tracks and one lone child chained to the other set of tracks in front of him, the purpose of the narrative in Job isn't to convey historical details. The purpose is to provoke us to examine what we believe.

Biblical scholars can help us see that it's best to think of the book of Job as an ancient, inspired thought experiment. Whether a historical person named "Job" lived through events like this is not important, just like whether or not the trolley car conductor was a historical person isn't pertinent to that story's purpose. The purpose of the book of Job is to get the ancient audience to think about the most righteous person they can imagine enduring the worst tragedies one could imagine befalling someone.[11]

Chapter one introduces us to the accusations of an angel called "the Challenger " (or *ha sa'tan* in Hebrew) in a sort of divine board meeting between God and His angelic court. Again we don't need to think of this as a description of something that historically happened. That's not how this genre of writing works. We also don't need to think of this challenging angel as the same Satan that we see throughout the New Testament (that may come as a shock to some of you, but there's good evidence that this is the case), nor do we need to take away from this story that God enters into wagers with Satan about the outcome of events. [12] Again, this is an inspired thought experiment.

In the opening scene of this inspired thought experiment,

the Challenger brings up two charges against the way God seems to have set up and governed the cosmos. First of all, is it really a good policy to have righteous people blessed for their righteousness? Doesn't that give people a selfish, ulterior motive for their righteousness, thereby undercutting righteousness altogether? Yet if righteous people suffer all the time, that seems like a really bad policy on God's part. After all, why be righteous if your life will be absolutely horrible anyway? [13] It's quite the *catch-22*.

The point here isn't that this is an actual angel's question in some angelic staff meeting that happened a long time ago; the point is that these provocations are giving voice to *Israel's questions* about how God governs the world. As I mentioned before, Israel's neighbors thought that the gods were petty in their grievances with humanity if humans failed to take care of their needs. If you did something wrong to upset the gods, you could expect to have some kind of evil befall you, either through the gods directly afflicting you or through gods merely leaving you alone and unshielded from the forces of primordial chaos. This entire system had nothing to do with the gods being just; it existed because the gods had mercurial temperaments and needs just like humans do. They were just more powerful.

As you comb through the Old Testament, you can see how an Israelite may be confused about whether or not this is how the one true God works. Consider the terms of God's covenant with Israel through Moses 'Law recorded in Deuteronomy:

> *"See, I set before you today life and prosperity, death and destruction. For I command you today to love the Lord your God, to walk in obedience to him, and to keep his commands, decrees and laws; then you will live and increase, and the Lord your God will bless you in the land you are entering to possess."* (Deuteronomy 30:15-16)

Follow God's commands, and God will bless you. On this

surface, you can see why this seems a bit like karma, but the complete picture of the Old Testament literature, including books like Job, makes this far more complex. Certainly, you have places such as the book of Psalms that are filled with songs where the Psalmist fully expects something like karma to work out for him. Take Psalm 26 or 35 as a couple of examples. There you can see the psalmist express full confidence that he will be vindicated and saved from injustice in the end because he's been righteous and held up his end of the covenantal deal with God. Over and over again, you see this idea that the righteous will get God's presence and the good perks that come with it, and the wicked will face the consequences of their evil choices. Good things happen to good people. Bad things happen to bad people.

Much of the book of Proverbs appears to affirm this retribution principle/karma concept as well, but when we read Psalms and Proverbs alongside other wisdom books like Job and Ecclesiastes, we begin to see that the short wisdom sayings of Proverbs aren't guarantees that if you follow them you're certain to get those results. These sayings of Proverbs are generalized truths that reveal the most normative pattern for how things typically work in the world. Another way of saying it is that *statistically* the wisdom of Proverbs will work out more times than not. If you have to choose to live your life a particular way, you should play those odds. Something akin to karma may generally be the norm, but that doesn't make it universally true in every instance.

This is what we see in the book of Job, with each of Job's friends arguing in differing ways that karma runs the world and that, in some sense, even God answers to karma. Job's friends represent the common responses people would give to the problem of evil in that cultural context, and when God shows up in the whirlwind after all of Job's friends are done talking, God silences them all. It is in God's lengthy discourse with Job, we learn how Israel's God is different from their cultural conceptions of God and how the people of God may need to reconsider their beliefs about suffering and evil (especially "natural" evils) in light of this true revelation.

First, if we want to know if God is "just," we should be careful not to impose a culturally conditioned notion of justice upon Him and then believe that He is bound to act in accordance with this justice. If "justice" is ontologically superior to that which we call "God," then "justice" is God. Instead, we need to understand that justice emanates from God's essence. God's just governance of the cosmos includes general norms for wise behavior that can look like karma at times, but make no mistake about it - karma does not run the universe. God does.

Secondly, *chaos* is not a primordial force beyond or before God. Many of Israel's ancient near eastern neighbors had creation myths that included violent struggles between the gods and some sort of personification of chaos or non-order. Ancient near eastern mythologies even had chaos-monsters. These chaos-monsters were Godzilla-like creatures who may not have been sinister or malevolent but were uncontrollable and brought destruction to the cosmos. Two of these well-known chaos-monsters were Leviathan and Behemoth. Israelites tended to stay away from the sea because of the mythical sea dragon known as Leviathan. There were good questions among Israel's neighbors as to whether these chaos-monsters could even take down gods, but here in Job, God dispels the mythical misconception that Leviathan is a threat to Him. In fact, in some paradoxical sense, non-order may actually be designed into the cosmos (I will propose a reason *why* in our concluding chapters). Job might not be able to take down this symbolic Godzilla, but the task isn't beyond God.[14]

Third, not all suffering can be linked directly to someone's sin or foolishness. While suffering can be the result of sinful *dis-order* (I've hyphenated dis-order intentionally for purposes that will become clear later in this book), it may also be the case that suffering is experienced as part of encountering the not-yet-fully ordered, or that suffering in this age is part of the right-ordering of the cosmos in the wisdom of God. Either way, the book of Job demonstrates that people don't always get what they deserve.

What if the world was governed by karma instead of God? What if everyone always got what they "deserved" from their actions? Is that really the kind of world we want to live in, a world where there is no room for grace or mercy? Perhaps the cost of designing a creation with room for the possibility of grace, mercy, and forgiveness of sins is that righteous people like Job won't always get what they deserve. After all, isn't that at the core of the Christian message? There was none more righteous than Jesus of Nazareth, and thereby none more undeserving of the agonizing, unjust suffering of the Cross. But what do Christians believe about the Cross? That the Cross was God's demonstration of grace towards the world.

> "But God demonstrates his own love for us in this: While we were still sinners, Christ died for us." (Romans 5:8)

We will revisit this idea of God designing a world that allows for mercy and grace in the concluding chapters of this book, but for now our tour must continue onward by exploring some of the tensions in the biblical literature between the Old Testament and New Testament surrounding God's role in evil and suffering.

3. TENSIONS BETWEEN THE TESTAMENTS

Remember that hypothetical question I asked earlier about what is the most biblical response to hearing a diagnosis that a loved one has come down with a debilitating disease? Doesn't it sometimes seem that the answer would vary between whether you're reading the Old Testament a lot that week or reading something in the New Testament like the Gospels or the book of Acts? It's okay to be honest about this tension we feel when we read the Bible cover to cover.

In the Old Testament, God seemingly accepts regular culpability for suffering-inducing events, many of which we might normally label as "evil" if we weren't ever-so-slightly concerned about this God smiting us too for saying such a thing. Sometimes God explicitly claims responsibility for events that cause significant suffering and death, such as the plague that killed all the firstborns in Egypt (Exodus 11:1-12:36). If, like me, you grew up watching *The Ten Commandments* with Charleton Heston, you might remember that final plague as being performed by the "angel of death." But like many things in that movie, that isn't what the Bible actually says. No, Yahweh takes specific credit for the death of the Egyptian children.

It's not that death angels don't ever get called into the service of God in the Old Testament. You also had the scene recorded in 2 Kings 19, where the angel of death lays waste to

185,000 men in Sennacherib's Assyrian army. That is a lot of death. Of course, it's not just spiritual moral agents that carry out violent acts as an apparent extension of God's will; it's also human moral agents. Consider how God calls the Babylonian king Nebuchadnezzar- the king who lays waste to the city of Jerusalem, killing untold numbers of God's covenant people- "my servant" (Jeremiah 27:6).

We can be honest about how at odds these passages can feel with what we read when we make our way through the Gospels at the beginning of the New Testament. As I mentioned before, the New Testament contains 568 references to Satan or the demonic, but in contemporary Jewish theology, which is based exclusively on the Hebrew Bible (what Christians commonly call the Old Testament), "Satan plays virtually no role."[15] In the New Testament, this *diabolos*, Devil or Satan, appears to be an individual spiritual moral agent atop the hierarchy of evil in the cosmos.

Sometimes this Satan is referred to as Beelzebub, from *Baal Zebub* or the "lord of the flies" worshiped by the Philistines in the Old Testament. [16] Other times he's referred to as prince or ruler of this world, the evil one, and is even associated with a dragon in the book of Revelation. He tempts Jesus in the wilderness, causes instances of sickness and disease, and enters Judas when he's about to betray Jesus. In John's Gospel, just before Jesus heads to the Cross, Jesus claims His work on the cross was an act of judgment on the prince of this world (John 12 & 16). The epistle of 1 John claims that "the devil has been sinning from the beginning. The reason the Son of God appeared was to destroy the devil's work."(1 John 3:8)

Luke writes in Acts 10 a summarization of Jesus's mission as, "God anointed Jesus of Nazareth with the Holy Spirit and power, and how he went around doing good and healing all who were under the power of the devil, because God was with him." The apostle Paul believes Satan is behind the world's corrupt human powers and even sees him as obstructing his missionary ventures at times. [17] What is to account for this change of emphasis? Is there any way to harmonize these seemingly disparate pictures in the Old and New Testament in a way that can help us meaningfully address our questions about the problem of evil and give us a guide for how to respond appropriately to incidents of suffering?

Before we do that, it may be helpful to understand what happened historically in Jewish religious literature between the Old and New Testaments. In the 1940s, the discovery of the Dead Sea Scrolls completely revolutionized our understanding of the ancient biblical world. The Dead Sea Scrolls are a collection of religious scrolls found in the Qumran Caves of the Judean desert that date back to the 3rd century BC up to AD 70. Not only did these remains of ancient manuscripts include glimpses into books in the Old Testament canon, but they also included new intertestamental books that can help us see the evolution of Jewish thought on things like angels, demons, and the after-life.

At least in this particular community in Qumran, there was a strong affinity for apocalyptic stories- stories that portrayed an imminent, final conclusion to the struggle between the forces of good and evil.[18] Several of these apocalyptic stories frame the problem of evil as being about a cosmic battle between spiritual powers, with fallen angels and demons responsible for leading humanity astray. [19] The term *fallen angels* presumes some type of celestial fall event, but there is no explicit angelic-rebellion backstory in the Old Testament. Some may point to Genesis 6:1-4, but it is far from explicit unless you let these intertestamental, apocalyptic stories shape your perspective.

Two of the most important books from this era discovered in the Dead Sea Scrolls are 1 Enoch and the book of Jubilees. 1 Enoch was likely written sometime in the 3rd century BC with possibly some later edits, and it tells the story of the "Watchers" or "Sons of God" rebelling against God as they lust after human women. This is the supposed backstory for that peculiar Genesis

6:1-4 passage. Yes, it is weird and wild, but it only gets more peculiar. This story claims these fallen angels have children with human women, producing a race of violent giants called the *Nephilim* who threaten to destroy creation. [20]

There's also a second cosmic backstory in Enoch, and in this fall-of-the-angels backstory, the author claims that the fallen angels taught men how to make weapons and use magic and that they taught women to wear make-up. I get how patronizing that sounds to women, but I'm not making this up (yes, pun intended).

In both of these backstories, there is a clear, singular leader of the fallen angels called Shemihaza or Asael. In light of the existential threat of the Nephilim and these fallen angels, humanity cries out to God for help. God responds by sending the flood and charges the archangels, Michael and Raphael, to bind Asael in Hades/Tartarus until an appointed day of judgment. The spirits of the dead Nephilim become the demons. The book of Jubilees essentially tells the same story but gives the additional detail that God allowed one-tenth of the giant spirits to remain because the leader of the fallen angels pleaded with God on their behalf. [21]

Why am I telling you all this? Is it because I believe these stories are inspired and authoritative just like the books we have in the canon of the Bible? Certainly not. However, I do believe that understanding these stories found in the Dead Sea Scrolls is important because they help us understand how the Jewish worldview shifted and evolved between the Old Testament and New Testament. In fact, we can see quite a bit of explicit evidence in the New Testament that intertestamental books like Enoch played a role in shaping the New Testament authors 'and audience's understanding of evil, angels, demons, and God's will in the cosmos.

Take, for example, Matthew 25:41 and this line about the "eternal fire prepared for the devil and his angels." We may just gloss over an expression like that out of familiarity and not think much about it. Pretty standard day of judgment lingo, right? But could you find this idea that there is a final judgment to come on the devil and his angels anywhere in the Old Testament? You can search for yourself, but you won't find it.[22] So why isn't anyone in attendance at Jesus 'class on the final judgment that day raising their hand and saying, "Umm...Rabbi, what's this stuff about the devil and his angels and the eternal fire prepared for them? I've never heard of that at synagogue?" One likely reason is because of the intertestamental apocalyptic literature, which explicitly describes scenes just like this. We know that the book of Jude quotes from the first book of Enoch and the Testament of Moses, so we can see that at least some of these stories were viewed as important even if they were not sacred Scripture. [23]

So what are we to make of these apparent differences between the Old and New Testament as we try to find answers to our questions about evil and suffering? There are several differing interpretative approaches that people take. One approach is to place a primary hermeneutic emphasis on those Old Testament scripture texts that seem to suggest that God is causally responsible for all things- evil and suffering included. Another approach might be to see God as needing to accept an extra-helping of responsibility for evil and suffering in the Old Testament in order to pull Israel out of their cultural temptation toward polytheism. All of Israel's neighbors were polytheists, with rival gods often competing for power and authority in the divine realm of the gods. If God reveals to Israel early on in their history the sort of things revealed about Satan and demons in the New Testament, then perhaps Israel would become tempted to see Satan as a rival god.

A third approach may be to see God working in Israel's cultural neighbors, especially during Israel's exile years and into the Second Temple period, to progressively reveal things about himself and the nature of reality to Israel that they had not fully understood before. Historically, we can see strong evidence of new theological and philosophical developments after Israel's exile in Babylon. Ideas such as postmortem judgment, the resurrection of the dead, more dualistic theodicies postulating a cosmic struggle between good and evil, and even body-soul dualisms aren't features of Israel's worldview until the exile and post-exilic period (i.e., after the 6th century BC). [24]

A fourth interpretive approach may be to see God's acceptance of responsibility for instances of evil and suffering in the Old Testament and the lack of revelatory disclosure about Satan and demons in the New Testament as part of an intentional revelatory strategy on God's part designed to protect the Old Testament people of God from fearing what they were powerless to confront. Before the incarnation, death, and resurrection of Jesus, and the subsequent empowerment of the Holy Spirit, humanity was powerless to do anything about Satan, demons, and malevolent principalities and powers. Only in the God-Man, Jesus Christ was there victory over the powers of darkness. In this interpretative approach, the New Testament gives us a more complete picture because the people of God in Christ are now capable of not living in fear of Satan as they would have been before Christ's victorious work.

Certainly, there are other interpretative approaches that people take to try and make a coherent theodicy out of their reading of the Bible. There may be potential issues you have with each of the four I listed above. There may be a particular approach or combination of approaches that may appeal to you. Either way, I am not going to attempt to settle which interpretative approach (or approaches) is best quite yet. We'll save that until the concluding chapters of this book.

Part of what we want to be able to do before we land on a particular interpretive approach or come to any other sort of theological conclusion is to compare our initial findings with Christians who have gone before us. Can we trace our theological beliefs back through the ages to see if they have historical predecessors? Can we connect those historical predecessors to others who have gone before them? How far back can we trace them? Can we go all the way back to the earliest Christians who wrote, collected, and preserved the New Testament canon of Scripture? Can we pinpoint specific moments in history where the theology diverged from those who came before? What caused it? Who's in the right?

These are the sorts of good investigative questions we want to have in mind as we consider or reassess what we believe about God, evil, and suffering. As we work our way through centuries of church history and compare the sometimes complementary and sometimes divergent theodicies of some of the most brilliant Christian minds, I want to invite you to keep a mental or written list of the responses each voice from the past may give to some of your more pressing questions about God, evil, and suffering. [25]

PART II- COMPARING HISTORICAL PERSPECTIVES:
CLASSIC PERSPECTIVES

4. EARLY CHRISTIAN VOICES & GNOSTICISM: IS OUR WORLD FUNDAMENTALLY EVIL?

From the very beginning, followers of this new Way of Jesus gathering in what would become known as "Christian" communities faced real challenges that threatened their continued existence. First, there were the Roman authorities and the local Jewish puppet government in Palestine. Second, there was the theological threat of what the Apostle Paul sometimes referred to as the "party of circumcision," who was demanding that new Greek, Roman, and other Middle Eastern and Mediterranean non-Jewish followers of Jesus act ethnically Jewish in order to be accepted as faithful followers of God. We see the early church's debates about this controversy in books like Romans and Galatians as prime examples. Finally, as we approach the end of the first century and the original Apostles begin to die out, a new threat emerges- a dangerous molotov cocktail of peculiar theological ideas and Greco-Roman philosophies that attracted many people still perplexed by the problem of evil. This counter-Christian movement that claimed to be the true message of Christianity is known today as Gnosticism.

Most of our remaining writings from this late first century and second century period come from orthodox

Christian leaders addressing either the Gnostic controversy or other ideas that they felt threatened the New Testament Christianity of the original Apostolic witness. It's not as if we have Church Fathers writing specific treatises on evil and suffering in this era like we see in later periods in history. Still, as we get to know some of these early Church Fathers and the Gnostic heresies, we will see how some of the earliest Christians outside of the New Testament dealt with the problem of evil. In the process of doing that, we'll also see why Gnosticism was not only an appealing theodicy in the past, but we'll begin to understand how some of the Gnostics' ideas about evil and suffering continue to re-emerge throughout history and into the present.

Ignatius of Antioch was one of the earliest known Church Fathers after the New Testament apostles. Ignatius lived from approximately 35- 105 AD. He was a disciple of John the Beloved, who, according to church tradition, was not only the lone disciple in attendance at Jesus' crucifixion but allegedly survived being boiled alive in a cauldron of burning hot oil after refusing to recant his faith in Christ. [26] As an early convert to this new Way of Jesus, Ignatius would have been mentored by one of Jesus's closest friends. Scholars contest some of the writings attributed to Ignatius, but it is largely agreed upon that Ignatius wrote seven letters or epistles to early Christians in the late first to early second century. These letters give us access to some of the earliest known Christian writings outside the New Testament.

For Ignatius, the devil played a significant role in the evils of this present age. Ignatius calls Satan "the prince of this age" and blames heresy, disruption of Christian community, temptation to sin, and even people losing their faith on the activity of Satan. Again, at this point in history, Christians do not have the great luxury of being able to write comprehensive systematic theologies or entire books on the problem of evil. They are just trying to make it as a persecuted and often divided community, so it should be no surprise that when we read Ignatius that the kinds of evils he's most concerned about are the evils that seem to disrupt Christian community. For Ignatius, there were deep concerns that Christians could fall for demonic deception and give up on the true faith of the apostles. He warned Christians not to "be anointed with the bad odor of the devil's doctrine." Ignatius was eventually martyred for his faith, thrown to the lions- quite possibly even in the Roman Colosseum. [27]

Polycarp of Smyrna was another of our earliest known Christian leaders outside the New Testament apostles. Like Ignatius, he was also a disciple of John. He was born in 88 and was eventually martyred in 156 (dates of his death vary) for not recanting his faith or giving an offering of incense to the cult of the Roman Emperor. Unfortunately, we don't have much writing from Polycarp that would unlock a tremendous amount of insight into his thoughts on the problem of evil. We do know that Polycarp believed that false teachers who denied Christ's resurrection and the final judgment were the "first born of Satan," but we also know Polycarp did not see the malevolent agency of Satan in the world as a genuine rival to Christ's authority. All things in heaven and earth are subject to Christ, the Lord and final judge of all. Polycarp clearly believed that his own suffering, persecution, and grizzly execution were not purely the result of a demonic attack. In fact, Polycarp appeared to believe that his martyrdom was, in some sense, a good gift. "I bless you Father for judging me worthy of this hour, so that in the company of the martyrs I may share the cup of Christ." These were among Polycarp's final words before Roman guards ran him through with a spear, frustrated that the flame they had set to consume him before the crowds did not seem to be killing him.[28]

Christian writers in the second century continued to address heretical teaching and internal church controversies, but as Christianity continued to spread throughout the Roman

Empire, Christian leaders also began to give more focused attention to apologetic defenses of the faith to help those who were not Christian better understand the basic tenets of Christian theology. Doing this became increasingly difficult when rival explanations of the Christian story would spring up and claim to be the true meaning of Jesus 'life and message.

∗ ∗ ∗

There were several significant movements of Gnostic Christianity at this time, which despite their subtle variations, all shared a hyper-dualistic vision of reality. The radical dualism of these Gnostic sects seemed to offer a compelling narrative for people to live in. Oftentimes when Christians learn about early Gnosticism in a church history class or Sunday school lesson, the focus tends to be on how some of these gnostic groups preached that salvation is achieved through accessing secret knowledge about God and reality. While there is undoubtedly some truth to this, focusing on this aspect of Gnosticism makes it difficult to understand why so many people found it compelling. One of the biggest reasons gnostic systems were so persuasive is that they seemed to offer a clear answer to the problem of evil. To help us understand how the Gnostics offered an enticing theodicy, let's start by looking at one particular example of a Gnostic theology in the form of the third-century gnostic named Mani.

Born in April of 216, Mani demonstrated at an early age an interest in theology, cosmology, and mystic philosophy. While still a young man, Mani claimed to have an encounter with a spirit that he believed to be a twin form of his divine self. This spirit supposedly revealed to Mani the secret knowledge needed for salvation. Mani went on to claim to be the "advocate" and "comforter" promised by Jesus and saw himself as the final prophet in a line of prophets that included Zoroaster, Plato, the Buddha, and Jesus.[29] Drawing upon a popular vision of reality taught by Plato, Mani believed that reality was split into two fundamental principles of matter and spirit. For Mani, these were opposing principles that he compared to light and darkness, heaven and hell.

In the beginning, creation was ruled by Light, but at some point, the Devil stumbled upon the border dividing the Light and the Dark and tried to conquer the Light. God the Father responded to this insurrection by calling upon the spirits that emanated from himself to go to war with the Devil and his demons. In this cosmic collision, some of the Light was trapped within the evil matter. This Light trapped within Matter formed the human soul, so humans, like the rest of the cosmic order, are caught up in a struggle between the divine Light in their soul and the evil material Darkness of their flesh. The Light in their soul remains trapped in the evil matter until they awaken to the secret gnosis of God. The souls that do not attain enlightenment undergo an ongoing process of reincarnation until they eventually attain enlightenment.[30]

Manichaeism might seem strange to many of us today, but it was an enticing option for people because it offered what many perceived as a solution to the problem of evil. It did this by situating evil and suffering as an unintended catastrophe of a fundamental struggle between God and the Devil. Like other Gnostic systems, Manichaeism offered people a story that pitted good against evil and told them that they could one day escape all of the evil and suffering of the material world if they simply accessed the correct spiritual information.

Another example of a popular Gnostic theology was Marcionism. Marcionism began in the second century with the teachings of a man named Marcion. Marcion believed that Jesus was the Messiah and God sent Jesus to save the world. He affirmed the writings of the Apostle Paul but rejected the Old Testament/Hebrew Bible. Marcion believed that the God portrayed in the story of Israel throughout the Old Testament was a lesser god and a cruel tyrannical demiurge. Marcionism equated Yahweh of the Israelites with the lesser demiurge of Platonism responsible for the flawed creation of the material world. The true Supreme Being, or the *Monad*, was the good God who sent Jesus into the world.

Marcion's Jesus wasn't the orthodox picture of Christ held by the rest of the Church and portrayed in the Gospels. This Jesus wasn't material at all, as to be material would mean that he was a product of the evil demiurge. Marcion's Jesus was only spirit, and his salvation was an offering of spiritual enlightenment necessary to release human souls from the wicked material world of the Demiurge. Marcion went on to curate his own version of the Biblical canon, which had only eleven books and most famously excluded the entire Old Testament. [31]

I have taken the time to highlight these two Gnostic theologies not to give you merely a fascinating history lesson but to help you identify when variations of these ideas crop up in contemporary Christianity... because they do! Gnostic-infused "evangelism" strategies can borrow from Marcion and Mani and promise an escape from the suffering of our material world into the sweet by-and-by through accepting the right information about God hidden from the rest of the world. I even remember the first time I watched *The Matrix* in 1999 and thought it was a brilliant Christian parable- Neo trapped in an evil, illusory material world run by malevolent principalities, needing access to secret knowledge in order to be liberated from the Matrix. It's hard to get more Gnostic than that! If we merely rage against the machine and see that there is no spoon, we can be freed from our suffering. But as early responders to the Gnostic heresies such as Justin Martyr, Ireneaus, and Tertullian demonstrated, the Gnostic solution to the problem of evil via a hyper-dualistic view of reality and secret, spiritual escapism was no real solution at all.

5. JUSTIN MARTYR & IRENAEUS: IS SATAN A RIVAL TO GOD?

The early Gnostic heresies focussed on a hyper-dualistic vision of reality caught up in a cosmic struggle between forces of good and evil. If you were living in the second or third century, you likely had far greater first-hand exposure to instances of moral and natural evil than most middle-class Americans do today. The material world did seem like an often inhospitable place you had to conquer. How could a good God ever be responsible for a world this broken? Living in the ancient Roman Empire meant a life of expectancy of 20-33 years old. If you factor out infant and child mortality, you might live to see 40 or 50 years old. [32] This can't all be God's doing, can it?

The most important theologian of the second century, Justin Martyr, vehemently denied what we might call the *hyper ontological dualism* of the Gnostics (meaning the belief that reality itself is fundamentally comprised of rival forces of good and evil) while simultaneous denying *monistic theodicies* which would pin all that happens in the world, including all evil and suffering, on God as the singular causal source. While Justin wasn't primarily concerned with addressing the problem of evil, his work, which focuses on giving a defense of orthodox Christian theology to a suspicious Roman emperor and the philosophers of his day, does end up giving us relevant insights into Justin's theodicy, as well as what may have been normative, orthodox Christian attitudes towards the causal forces behind evil and suffering.

In continuity with what appeared to be the consensus among Christian writers of the first century, Justin Martyr's own position might be called *moderate cosmic dualism*. Whereas the hyper-dualist Gnostics saw the building blocks of reality split between opposing forces of good and evil, Justin's *moderate cosmic dualism* affirmed a real collision *within* the cosmic arena between forces of good and evil but rejected the Gnostic idea that behind creation itself were powerful malevolent forces or a demonic demiurge. For Justin, Satan led a very real rebellion within the cosmos against God, but only because God temporarily allowed him to sow his evil and suffering.

Justin believed these wicked spirits were once angels assigned the task of caring for God's creation but eventually rebelled against their vocational calling. In keeping with a popular intertestamental era view found in the non-canonical book of Enoch (and hinted at in Genesis 6 among other places in the Bible), Justin also believed that before the Noahic Flood, some fallen angels became "captivated by love of women and begat children, who are those that are called demons."[33]

I know at this point some of you are cringing. That's probably an appropriate response. Others of you who have ever taken an ill-advised, late-night YouTube surf for the keyword *Nephilim* are probably chuckling right now. Whatever your reaction, don't throw out all of what Justin Martyr has to say because of this. Like it or not, as I mentioned in chapter 2, this was a pretty common perspective among Christians for centuries. I will personally refrain from making a value judgment on this subject, but the more important point in bringing all of this up is to highlight how seriously Justin takes the influence of demonic forces in affecting the amount of evil and suffering in our world. Justin does this while rejecting the Gnostic idea of a competing, incompetent, or malevolent demiurge being behind the created, material world. For Justin, the existence of a cosmic struggle where evil and suffering exist is simply the side effect of God's intentional choice to create a world where moral agents, both human and angelic, have free will.

Why God chose to create a world where the possibility of moral agents rejecting his will exists is a puzzle that Justin does not attempt to solve fully. What Justin does give is a hopeful vision for the eventual ending of all evil and a defense for why God delays in bringing this end about.

> "that [Satan] would be sent into the fire with his host, and the men who follow him, and would be punished for an endless duration . . . the reason why God has delayed to do this, is His regard for the human race. For He fore-knows that some are to be saved by repentance, some even that are perhaps not yet born. In the beginning He made the human race with the power of thought and of choosing the truth and doing right, so that all men are without excuse before God; for they have been born rational and contemplative." [34]

That God doesn't immediately bring the human story to an end is due to his love for humanity and his desire for the maximum opportunity for repentance, even allowing for those who have yet to be born to be able to enter into loving communion with Him.

Though Justin Martyr was arguably the most important Church Father of the second century, the importance of another second-century Church Father named Irenaeus should not be overlooked. Irenaeus lived from 135-202, and like Justin, he railed against the Gnostic heresies of their day. Like Justin, Irenaeus could also be classified as a *moderate cosmic dualist,* taking seriously the influence of Satan in perpetuating evil and suffering in the cosmic order while not assigning so much weight to his power as to make him an ontological rival to God like the hyper dualists.

✱✱✱

Irenaeus believed that the Devil was once a good angel made by God who rebelled against God. While biblical scholars debate whether there is satisfactory evidence to claim that this backstory has any biblical precedent, we could say, at the very least, that there certainly is not an explicit fall-of-Satan backstory in the Bible. Ireneaus also makes another connection that isn't explicitly in the biblical text but consequently garners a considerable amount of acceptance among Christians throughout the rest of Christian history. Ireneaus believed that the serpent in the Garden of Eden was Satan- a point of interpretation that isn't ludicrous but also is not explicitly stated in Genesis either. Because Satan initiated the deception of the primordial couple, God's curse was not primarily aimed at the humans but at Satan. Humans fall for Satan's deception because "man was a child, not yet having his understanding perfected; wherefore also he was easily led astray by the deceiver."[35]

It was part of God's necessary plan that humans should enter the world like naive, uneducated children and go through a process of maturing towards perfection. How does humanity come to grow into God's intended perfection and triumph over Satan and evil? Irenaeus believed this happened through Jesus as true God and true human succeeding where the primordial couple failed.

> "He has therefore, in His work of recapitulation, summed up all things, both waging war against our enemy, and crushing him who had at the beginning led us away captives in Adam, and trampled upon

his head...in order that, as our species went down to death through a vanquished man, so we may ascend to life again through a victorious one; and as through a man death received the palm [of victory] against us, so again by a man we may receive the palm against death."[36]

Like Justin, Irenaeus taught that Satan is only allowed a temporary dominion by God and that Satan cannot override human free will. As moral evils go, Satan can only tempt people towards evil, but humans are fully capable of rejecting those temptations. The wrath of God's judgment is primarily directed towards the Devil, but those who succumb to Satan's temptations and align themselves with Satan's rebellion will meet the same end if they do not repent.

It is clear from the work of the first and second-century Church Fathers that early Christians were not as monistic in their theodicy as early Hebraic thought and yet were also not as dualistic as the Gnostics. They believe Satan was a real moral agent, a fallen angel, even a "prince of this world" able to deceive, physically afflict people, and move governing powers to persecute the church, but he is never a rival to God. The material world isn't evil, and the goal isn't to escape it. One other important takeaway from this time period, especially in light of Marcionism, is that these early Christians firmly believed that the Old and New Testaments were part of one unified, cohesive story and that there was only one good God behind it all. Evil, both moral and natural, is the result of human and angelic moral agents misusing their will.

Now admittedly, these early Church Fathers weren't setting out to write treatises on the problem of evil and were much more focussed on the moral evils and spiritual threats that attempted to disrupt Christian community than trying to explain the causes for natural evils like pandemics and natural disasters. Acknowledging this, we can still deduce some relevant beliefs to our questions about evil and suffering from the writings of these early Church Fathers.

Once again, it is clear that early Christianity was not as monistic in its theodicy as Judaism and not as dualistic as Gnosticism. Those appear to be the boundary markers of orthodox Christian theodicy early on. The Gnostics were a fierce competitor because they offered what appeared on the surface to be an easy answer to people's questions about the natural evils and suffering they so frequently experienced in the ancient world. Matter and the natural world were just fundamentally evil. All you needed to do was escape it. Yet the early Christian message clearly denied this escapism. God made creation and the material world as inherently good. Angelic and human moral agents have misused their will, by their own volition, to bring dis-order into God's good creation. Satan and his fallen angels were the first to do so and tempted humanity to do the same. Who or what tempted Satan first is a question no early Christian writer gives an answer for, but there is universal consensus on Satan's culpability in his fall.

You get the sense from some of these early Fathers that Satan had deceived and kidnapped humanity, and while humanity is responsible for not heeding God's instructions and falling for Satan's deceptions, God's wrath is primarily directed toward the kidnapper, not the kids. In Christ, God ransomed humanity from the dominion of Satan. Through baptism and Christian practices like prayer, Christians can resist Satan as he is ultimately a defeated foe whose final judgment has not yet come.

God was in the process of redeeming the good creation He had made, and He would bring a final judgment upon all evil and resurrect the righteous to inherit the world they partnered with God in redeeming. This partnership with God did not deliver you from all suffering. In fact, the early Christian writers make evident that Christians should even expect to share in Christ's sufferings in this life. Sharing in Christ's suffering should not be considered an act of judgment, but we should also not rule out that God may be active in bringing temporary, painful consequences for sinful behavior so that our appetites for sin may be curbed.

6. ORIGEN & GREGORY OF NYSSA: WHAT IS GOOD & EVIL?

From the third through the fifth century, three brilliant and controversial theologians proposed responses to the problem of evil that would become the standard answers theologians and philosophers would refer to for centuries after. These three men were Origen, Gregory of Nyssa, and Augustine (who I will cover in the following chapter). To understand the theology of each of these three men, we need to understand more about the prevailing philosophical worldview of their era.

Just as it is central to our modern understanding of the world to believe in the laws of gravity or thermodynamics, Platonism and the emerging Neoplatonism of the third through the fifth century were effectively the scientific worldview of their day. Some of the beliefs of these three men will appear very strange and maybe even heretical at times, but we must understand that within their time and context, the Platonic/Neoplatonic view of the world was as settled as Albert Einstein's theory of relativity is to us today.

To give an extensive history of the philosophy of the classical Athenian philosopher Plato would be a detour far too distracting to the purposes of this book, but the way that Origen, Gregory of Nyssa, Augustine, and subsequent generations of Christian theologians and philosophers attempt to address the problem of evil will make very little sense unless we have, at the very least, a basic snapshot of this complex worldview. To give you the most appropriate snapshot of the era that Origen, Gregory of Nyssa, and Augustine lived in, let's focus more precisely on the Neoplatonism that emerged from the work of the Platonic philosopher, Plotinus.

Though technically Plotinus 'work would have likely had little direct effect on Origen as Origen was nearly 20 years older than Plotinus, Plotinus 'work best represents the steady evolution in Platonic thought happening during that time and can still give us a reliable snapshot into the predominant philosophical worldview of the larger Roman world in the third century. Plus, there is some evidence that Origen and Plotinus studied under the same teacher, which, if true, would give us an even stronger reason to believe that by understanding Plotinus we may have a better understanding of Origen's worldview. [37]

Like Plato, Plotinus taught that there was a transcendent One who was beyond all categories or classifications of being or non-being. The One was not personal like the Jewish and Christian conceptions of God. The One was immutable, unchangeable, and impassible. The One was the first cause of *being* itself. All reality emanates from the fundamental, pure light of the One. Within Neoplatonism, you had a hierarchical ordering of these emanations from the One. The first and closest emanation from the pure light of the One was the *Nous*, or as the Stoics called it centuries before, the *Logos*. This Nous or Logos was the reason, order, and intelligibility of reality itself. We could consider this Nous/Logos as the first-born of the One, not in the sense of being born first in a sequence of time, but in it being fundamental to the structure of the rest of reality. [38]

The next emanation in this hierarchical structure of reality was the *World Soul*, which emanates from the Nous/Logos. With each new level of emanation, you get further and further away from the One, also known as the *Good*. Matter was so far down the emanation ladder and so far away from the Good that it was filled with chaotic potentiality instead of inherent order and beauty. This potentiality could be transformed out of chaos into some *thing* by being formed, or more specifically, *informed*. Plop the right information into inorganic chaotic potentiality, and *viola-* you get an organic living thing. Put even more of the right information into this low-level organic thing, and you can get a higher-level rational creature. So the goal for the human mind was to be properly formed with the right information in order to have its will turned towards the One.

What is evil then within this Neoplatonic worldview? Evil is the disorganization and chaos that emerges as a result of movement away from the Good. The further away something moves from the Good as the source of all life, the closer it approaches a state of complete non-being. Think of it as a movement away from a light source to increasing darkness until you get to the point of the complete absence of visibility. The hotbed of Platonic and Neoplatonic philosophy was the city of Alexandria, home of Christianity's first great systematic theologian and the first teacher of biblical hermeneutics, Origen.

✳ ✳ ✳

Origen of Alexandria lived from 185-254 and is one of the most fascinating and controversial theologians in Christian history. He set the standard for biblical interpretation all the way until the Protestant Reformation well over a millennium later. He was frequently invited to important synods to eloquently take down heresies, and yet was also accused in his lifetime and in the centuries that followed of being a heretic. Forgers penned faked transcripts of his speeches, sending them to the Bishop of Rome to incriminate him for speculative questions about whether God's forgiveness could ever be extended to even Satan himself. While Origen certainly asked speculative questions (haven't all of us ever sat in Sunday school and silently mulled over that question?), his enemies falsely claimed to the Bishop that Origen was teaching the salvation of

Satan as settled doctrine.[39]

Origen's work was of monumental importance because he attempted, as all significant Christian theologians and philosophers do, to work through the implications of the biblical narrative within his unique cultural context. It just so happened that Origen's context was deeply Platonic and evolving into the newer forms of Neoplatonism I highlighted in the work of Plotinus. So as I outline Origen's theodicy, I want to encourage you to see it as being situated within the "science" of his day even if we would see that science as incorrect.

Origen believed that there were two acts of creation. The first was the creation of the spiritual domain or the "realm of pure intellects."[40] These pure intellects were the angelic beings whom God created with free will. These angelic beings differ from God in that they are able to go through the change of potentiality to actuality, whereas God is pure actuality with no potential to change. Some of these pure intellects or rational angelic beings use that potentiality to move away from God, who is the Good. Like Plotinus, Origen sees evil as a misuse of potentiality -a misuse of the will. Why did these angelic beings misuse their freedom of will and potentiality? Origen gives two possible causes but no real explanation as to why.

The first possibility is that the Devil as a moral agent fell first and tempted other angels, even attempting to deceive the pre-incarnate Son of God into rebellion. He was unsuccessful in deceiving the Son, but many angels fell for Satan's temptations. The second possibility Origen gives for the original movement of the angels away from the Good would make for a far less exciting movie. Origen wonders whether these angels just got lazy or bored and turned away.[41]

For the second act of creation, God created the material world. Unlike Gnosticism which taught that a lesser deity or wicked demiurge created our world, Origen believed that God created the material cosmos as a way of stopping the first fall from heading so far away from the Good that it would lead to the cessation of the first creation's existence. Souls were part of that first act of creation, so humans are created to receive a soul that can be rehabilitated and reoriented towards the Good. This was certainly a new perspective compared to our previous Church Fathers, and it's a perspective that I feel comfortable saying, even as I attempt to be a neutral tour guide, does not have justifiable biblical precedent; but once again, I'm also asking you to sympathetically consider that Origen is trying to give a deep cosmological explanation for the problem of evil that fits within the science of his day while still vociferously denying Gnosticism. In fact, we can see Plotinus argue a similar point about human souls:

> "The soul is a divine being and dwells in more heavenly places, but has entered the body. The soul is...a derivative aspect of the divine; but, compelled by its powers and due to its tendency to bring order to whatever is beneath it, it penetrates to this Lower Sphere [the material world] in a voluntary plunge."[42]

> "Just as Narcissus fell in love with his own image in the mirroring water... and fell into the water and drowned, so the souls of humans, seeing their images in the mirror of matter, have entered into the material world in a leap downward from the Supreme. Yet even they are not cut off from their origin, from the divine mind."[43]

As you can see, Origen was attempting to Christianize the Platonism/Neoplatonism of his day, and his most complicated challenge in the face of Gnosticism was to somehow come up with a way of affirming the goodness and value of the material world that Christians have traditionally affirmed. What are God's purposes for the material world? Origen uses a couple of different metaphors that may be helpful. The first of which is a picture of the material world as a school.[44] Evil and suffering are a part of our experience in this world, but they are instructive lessons in virtue so that our souls might be reoriented back to God.

The second picture Origen uses is that of a hospital. God created our world and gifted us with the experience of these flesh and blood lives so that our souls may be healed and rehabilitated. Evil and suffering will not always be, but if our souls are ever to be united with God in perfect union *while* retaining our free will, then we must be healed of our desires to move away from the Good so that one day, in the Age to Come, we will only ever use our will to be in harmony with God. Once we step back and perhaps set aside any disdain we may have for the Platonic/Neoplatonic philosophy in Origen's work, we might be able to see that there could be a compelling theodicy nestled within Origen's ideas.

After all, haven't most of us ever questioned how God will bring about a New Heavens and New Earth without evil and suffering and without us somehow losing our free will so we won't sin and rebel there too? If Origen is even partially right about this life being like a school or hospital, then maybe that's how. Perhaps human nature will be so transformed into Christ-likeness that any temptation towards even the slightest sin would be as appealing to us as a temptation to punch a baby in the face (we will revisit this idea in the concluding chapter of this book).

Origen is also famous for speculating as to whether or not there may one day be a final return of all rational intellects/souls into the original harmony of perfect contemplation of God. The theological term for this in Greek is *apokatastasis*, meaning "return" or "restoration." The logic in his reasoning is pretty consistent. If God made the material world as a hospital for the rehabilitation of souls, will God have failed if his hospital does not eventually heal all? This is why many consider Origen the first to propose what was later called *Christian universalism.*

***

Gregory of Nyssa (335-394) carried on much of the Origenian tradition. It is from Gregory and his brother Basil that we get the orthodox description of the Trinity as "one essence in three persons." Gregory was also instrumental in the formation of the Nicene Creed. In other words, Gregory is a guy setting the standards for what is orthodox Christian theology in the fourth century and beyond. By the time we reach the fourth century, Plotinus 'work has grown in importance. Gregory never directly quotes Plotinus, but like Origen, we can see Gregory attempt to defend the Christian story he received within this larger Neoplatonic worldview.

Unlike Origen, however, Gregory of Nyssa never attempted to offer a detailed cosmic backstory for Satan's fall, humbly exclaiming, "It is not part of my present business minutely to discuss." [45] This doesn't mean that Gregory was without opinion on Satan, evil, or suffering. Gregory believed that Satan's fall was because Satan "closed his eyes to the Good." [46] Once Satan closed his eyes to the Good and moved away from God, a malevolent momentum "propelled [him] with all his weight in the direction of vice."[47] On his trajectory further and further away from the Good, Satan attempted to corrupt humanity. His goal was to tempt humans with a perverted desire to "become [their] own murderer with [their] own hands."[48] But humanity was not inherently powerless against such temptation. Humans have the capacity of free will and can choose between good and evil, virtue and vice. Gregory echoes both Neoplatonic thought and Origen in describing evil not so much as a particular thing you choose but rather as the effects of a misused will. Without freedom of will, there can be no evil. "There is no such thing in the world as evil irrespective of a will," wrote Gregory. [49]

For Gregory of Nyssa, evil is not some independent reality as if you were at some all-you-can-eat buffet of moral choice and can choose between loading your plate with stuff from the good section or stuff from the evil section of the buffet. Instead, it would be like going to that all-you-can-eat buffet, taking all the food off the buffet line, and dumping it all over the floor. That would be a misuse of the intended good function of the food and the buffet. The food was not designed for that purpose, yet the potential exists for things not to be used for their good purpose. Evil is taking right-ordering and dis-ordering its proper purpose. Gregory believes that the intended good for humanity is union with God, but when humans misuse their potentiality for that good, the dis-ordered result is evil and unjust suffering. Gregory calls this a "retrocession of the soul from the beautiful."[50]

Okay, Greg, so answer me this- once that happened, why did God allow it to keep happening? I mean, as soon as Satan initially turned away from the Good, why not intervene and fix it right then and there? Gregory argued that once this initial movement away from God had started, God intentionally allowed it to reach "its utmost height" so that "when the healing remedy was applied it would pervade the whole of the diseased system."[51] Gregory believed that at the peak of the diseased system, Christ was sent into the world to bring about divine justice against Satan, and in keeping with the perspective of the early Church Fathers, to ransom us from Satan. Christ must be fully human and fully God so that "as with ravenous fish, the hook of the Deity might be gulped down along with the bait of flesh, and thus, life being introduced into the house of death and light shining in darkness, that which is diametrically opposed to light and life might vanish; for it is not in the nature of darkness to remain when light is present, or of death to exist when life is active."[52]

Similar to his predecessor Origen, Gregory of Nyssa believed, based on his interpretation of 1 Corinthians 15:28 where the Apostle Paul concludes his lengthy eschatological exposition by saying that in the end "God will be all in all," that all of the cosmos and every single human soul will one day be restored to unity with God. Gregory did not reject prior notions of judgment and hell; he simply believed that for Paul's words in 1 Corinthians to be true, hell must be a temporary purifying fire that burns away all that remains tempted to move away from God.

> "For it is evident that God will in truth be 'in all' when there shall be no evil in existence, when every created being is at harmony with itself, and every tongue shall confess that Jesus Christ is Lord; when every creature shall have been made one body. Now the body of Christ, as I have often said, is the whole of humanity...Neither is sin from eternity, nor will it last to eternity. For that which did not always exist shall not last forever."[53]

Neither Origen's nor Gregory of Nyssa's Christian universalism ever became the predominant mainstream view in Catholicism, Eastern Orthodoxy, or Protestant ism, and is considered heretical by many in each of these Christian traditions. It is not within the scope of this book to argue for the pros and cons of Christian universalism. Still, it is crucial to see how connected discussions of final judgment and salvation are to the problem of evil and suffering. For contemporary Christian philosophers like David Bentley Hart, Gregory of Nyssa's hope for ultimate reconciliation of all things is the only argument that can provide a satisfactory solution to why so much evil and suffering exists in a creation that a good God created out of nothing (*ex nihilo*).

Our next great Christian mind from the past would undoubtedly disagree with Hart. While drawing upon the work of our aforementioned predecessors, Augustine would differ on key points and establish the normative theological answers to difficult questions about evil and suffering in the Western tradition until this very day.

7. AUGUSTINE: BAD TO THE BONE

Augustine of Hippo (354-480) is the most influential and important theologian in church history. His theological journey began as a boy living in a household with a Roman pagan father and a Christian mother. Before becoming a Christian, Augustine was a Manichean. If you remember from our early chapter, Manichaeism was a Gnostic school of thought with a radically dualist theodicy. In one of Augustine's most important works, entitled *Confessions*, Augustine explained that the biggest appeal of this Gnostic philosophy was how it gave an easy answer to the problem of evil.[54] One of the things that Augustine initially found so appealing about Manichaeism was that in this worldview, individuals weren't truly responsible for evil as evil was part of the very nature of our material world. If evil is just baked into our flesh and bone bodies, what is there to feel guilty about?

But after a powerful conversion experience, Augustine turned away from Manichaeism. This doesn't mean that Augustine rejected all of the cultural inputs of his day. For any of us to do so is utterly impossible. Like Origen and Gregory of Nyssa before him, we can see the influence of Platonic and Neoplatonic thought in Augustine's writings. This should not cause us to dismiss his work where we see hints of Plato or Plotinus, as Christ is always working to reveal Himself to us through the cultures in which we are inextricably enmeshed. There is no culture-less Christianity. The difficult, nuanced work of good theologians of culture is to sift through the cultures we inhabit and to sort out what is both in keeping and out of place with God's revelation. Any truth that Plato or Plotinus had to share was only true because, whether intentional or not, it was in harmony with Christ as the fount of all truth, goodness, and beauty.

Augustine ultimately realized that there was far too much that was not in harmony with Christ about the gnostic Manicheans. Augustine believed that, among many problems, the Manicheans were asking the wrong question about evil. The primary question shouldn't be "what is the source of evil?" but rather "what is evil?"[55] For Augustine, evil is that which is contrary to something's God-ordered essence. "Evil is that which falls away from essence and tends towards non-existence."[56] Evil is the loss of good, and the loss of good creates pain and suffering. Obviously, you can see the influence of Neoplatonic language and the consistency between Augustine and Gregory of Nyssa on this understanding of what evil is. But do we need to completely throw out the Manicheans 'question of "what is the source of evil?"

> "God is the Good, and all things which He has made are good, though not so good as He who made them. For what madman would venture to require that the works should equal the workman, the creatures [equal] the Creator?"[57]

We can see an argument for what some might call the *metaphysical necessity of evil* in Augustine's writing. To put it another way, if God is perfectly good and God cannot create God, then by necessity there must be some distinction in goodness between Creator and creation. To imagine the perfection of truth, goodness, and beauty is to imagine God, so for there to be a Creator-creature distinction there has to be at least some degree of degradation between the creature and the Creator. Again, within a Neoplatonic frame (a frame that some would argue is not just Neoplatonic but also biblical), God has no potentiality as potentiality means the capacity to change. God gives his contingent creation potentiality, and moral agents misuse this potentiality to move away from Him. This obviously opens up a range of other questions that Augustine does not wish to give all of his time and attention to (but others in the future certainly address).

Augustine admits that he has no idea why that first movement away from God ever happened but argues that this first movement away from God had to be a defective movement on our part, not God's. God in his goodness will not allow that defective movement to continue onward in perpetuity and lead creation into non-being. Sounding like Origen and Gregory of Nyssa, Augustine wrote this in his *On the Morals of the Manicheans* in the year 388:

> "But the goodness of God does not permit the accomplishment of this end, but so orders all things that fall away that they may exist where their existence is most suitable, till in the order of their movements they return to that from which they fell away."[58]

In that same letter, Augustine also seems to express agreement with Origen's idea of pre-existent souls and that perhaps the soul's embodiment in flesh and bone was part of God's judgment- a perspective that he later clearly denounces when writing to the ancient church historian Jerome. By 397, we see clear shifts in Augustine's thought process that distance him from Origen and Gregory of Nyssa. Augustine wrestled with how the historic Christian belief that God created *ex nihilo* can square with his current understanding of what evil is. By 414, Augustine became embroiled in a series of hard-fought theological debates with rivals Pelagius and Bishop Julian of Eclanum, who supported Pelagius 'theology. Some of the central questions surrounding this debate were:

1) Are humans sinful and prone to misuse their will by their very nature?

2) If so, how? Would it be due to some already fallen pre-existent soul? Or is our inherent sinfulness somehow transferred to us from the first sinner Adam?

Pelagius taught that humans were created good by God and had the capacity to use their free will to either move towards the Good or away from it. In many ways, much of what Pelagius and his supporter Julian of Eclanum claimed didn't sound all that different from Gregory of Nyssa, Origen, or Justin Martyr. Augustine's concern emerged out of a logical question- if the will is free to move towards the Good then couldn't one, through a sheer act of will, move themselves to salvation and union with God? If so, what was the point of Jesus? And what would we make of the Scriptures written by the Apostle Paul that seemed to suggest that if you could have willed yourself into living in perfect alignment with God's commands, then the Law of Moses would have been sufficient?

Augustine's response to Pelagius and Julian of Eclanum became one of the most crucial theological moments in human history and carried massive implications for how every subsequent Christian generation attempted to address their deepest questions about evil, suffering, God's justice, hell, and more. In an effort to make a case for the logical necessity of Christ's work and to defend his understanding of Pauline theology, Augustine rebutted Pelagianism by teaching that humans inherit Adam's sinful soul hereditarily through the act of sexual procreation. Not to hastily move us from PG-13 territory to rated R territory, but it should be mentioned here that Augustine believed that the original sin of Adam is specifically passed on through the sperm of the man during sex.[59] Way to go, guys.

Because we are all biological descendants of Adam, we inherit through his seed an utterly depraved soul that is in need of saving. This depravity baked into our souls makes our wills incapable of actually choosing the Good. Our fundamental orientation is aimed toward evil, which makes the default destination of our eternal souls eternal damnation unless God's grace intercepts that trajectory away from God. If that happens, our souls experience a conversion from the kingdom of darkness to the Kingdom of Light and are regenerated with a new orientation towards God.

Julian fired back at Augustine and said he's reverting to his old Manichean ways.[60] If sin has contaminated even the material process by which humans are conceived, condemning humans even in the covenant of holy marriage to feel guilty for procreating little bundles of total depravity, then how is God's creation good at all? Even worse for Julian and his followers, it seemed like the implications of Augustine's theology were that a baby that died without the regeneration of their souls would be damned to hell. How is that kind of God good? And how is it just to bring every single person who ever lived into the world as already condemned sinners because one couple sinned? Doesn't this call into question the very goodness and justice of God?

In books 11 and 12 of Augustine's *City of God*, Augustine attempts to make clear that he completely rejects the sort of gnostic Manichean dualism that would turn all of creation into a fundamentally evil design. But if evil was not somehow fundamental to creation, then who or what tempted Satan and the first angels to fall? Augustine argues that the perversion of the will, whether it be Satan's will or human will, is not because of an external force but because of an inherent deficiency in the will itself, though we can have no explanation for why that deficiency exists. Again, maybe it comes down to the logically necessary difference between God that is pure actuality and a creation with potentiality. Without the potentiality to move away from the Good, creation would have no potentiality, and to have no potentiality and exist as pure actuality would be God. Creation cannot be God.

It is also in *City of God* that Augustine argues against Origen and Gregory of Nyssa's belief in Christian universalism. Earlier in his career when he was focused on arguing against the Gnostics, he appears to have agreed with Origen and Gregory of Nyssa on the possibility of the ultimate reconciliation of all things.[61] What changed his perspective, we cannot say for certain, but what is certain is the enduring impact of *City of God* on the rest of Christian theological history. Augustine still held to the science of his day that believed that souls were fundamentally immortal, but came to reject Origen & Gregory of Nyssa's claim that all souls will eventually be reconciled to God. He rejected this view based on his reading of Scripture, and in particular, what he thought was the clear teaching of Jesus in places like Matthew 25:41 on a final judgment that will sentence Satan and the wicked to eternal punishment in eternal fire.

Augustine also makes the case that because God exists outside of time (again a concept firmly accepted in the wider Platonic and Neoplatonic culture), God has eternally known what souls will be saved and what souls will not be saved. Not only that but God cannot be shocked by this information because there is no potentiality in God to receive new information and learn something. This means that God has intentionally determined all of human history. How this can be compatible with free will, which Augustine still defends, is a mystery that theologians and philosophers have debated since then. This view that God's predestination of all things is somehow compatible with human free will is called *compatibilism*.

Augustine remains to this day the most important theological pillar of the Christian tradition in the West, while

Gregory of Nyssa remains one of the most important pillars of the Christian tradition in the East. Augustine is revered in Catholic and Protestant circles alike, and his theology, including how he addressed questions related to evil, suffering, and God's will, is foundational for understanding the work of future theologians like Thomas Aquinas in the Middle Ages and Martin Luther and John Calvin during the Protestant Reformation.

As we begin to move out of the era of early Christian history and into the Middle Ages, now may be an appropriate time to assess the claims of each of the men we've discussed so far. Can you find connective threads that would link their theology back to the Scriptures? What questions have you brought into this book that you feel may have been adequately addressed by any of these voices from the past thus far? Have any of their views raised new questions or challenges you hadn't considered? That's okay too. Don't be discouraged. To do this journey well, we will want to compare notes from a variety of Christian perspectives from the past. If you've ever wrestled hard with any of these questions about God, evil, and suffering, chances are that you'll start to find that new questions arise just as you work your way through others. Again, this is good and healthy, even if it is difficult. Running away from our questions doesn't make them go away. So let's courageously press on!

8. THOMAS AQUINAS: A THEOLOGY OF EVERYTHING

The fall of Rome, to whom the Romans not-so-affectionately called "barbarians" in the year 410, sent shockwaves throughout Europe, North Africa, and Asia. You even have to wonder how much of the horrors of Rome's violent collapse played a role in Augustine's emphasis on the inherent sinfulness of human beings. At this point, the balance of the Empire's power was shifting eastward anyway. Constantine had already moved much of the political power to Constantinople nearly a century before (present-day Istanbul, Turkey). But there's no doubt that the West went through some dark years.

Three centuries after the fall of Rome, Charles the Great rose to power and united western and central Europe. Charles the Great had a deep value for education and Christian theology. During his reign, a bit of a renaissance of classical learning and preservation of ancient texts occurred. When Charles the Great died, Europe slowly descended into chaos, with kings and popes constantly fighting to fill the vacuum of power. Oh, and then you had that nasty little affair we call the Crusades where the forces of Christendom went to war with the powers of Islam. It wasn't Christianity's brightest moment.[62]

If you look back on the art and folklore from the High

Middle Ages, you notice that people had a pretty intense preoccupation with images of the devil, demons tormenting people, and all sorts of other depictions of darkness. Suppose you polled the average peasant in Europe living during this time with a medieval Family Feud-style survey question, "Who or what is responsible for evil and suffering in the world?" a medieval Sir Stephen Harvey would tell you that "the devil" would be the top answer on the board. But the average peasants' theodicy wasn't the same as the theodicy of the first or second-century Church Fathers who also assigned blame for evil and suffering on Satan. This was a much more superstitious rendition.

Did your girlfriend dump you for the stud archer in the king's army? It wasn't you. It was probably a demon. Not happy about the Muslims controlling Jerusalem, or that they even exist at all? Demons. When the plague known as the "black death" broke out in the 14th century, many blamed it on "demonic" Jews.[63] Yikes. Charlene Burns lays this out in much more detail in her book *Christian Understandings of Evil: The Historical Trajectory*.

Suffice to say that while the medieval period doesn't completely deserve the term the "Dark Ages", it wasn't entirely unwarranted. But even with all of this darkness, Christians created stunning works of art and timeless cathedrals. They built thriving universities like Oxford and Paris. In these universities, a new openness to learning from extra-biblical sources of wisdom was celebrated as part of the theological endeavor. They celebrated that we not only have God's revelation in the Scriptures as a guide, but we also have God's gift of reason or general revelation to enlighten us on who He is and the way His world works. This school of Christian thought became known as scholasticism, and the greatest scholastic theologian who ever lived was a man who attempted to give a theology of everything, including the problem of evil. His name was Thomas Aquinas.

Thomas Aquinas (1225-1274) is one of the most influential thinkers in history. Influenced by both Aristotle and the Christian tradition, Aquinas wrote one of the most ambitious works of theology in human history called *Summa Theologica*. While the secular atheism we are most familiar with in the 21st century did not exist in the 13th century, there have always been questions about how one could prove the existence of God, especially considering the challenges that the problem of evil poses to claims of an all-good and all-powerful God. Aquinas believed that despite the problem of evil, the existence of God was provable and famously devised five rational proofs for the existence of God. They were:

1) **The argument from motion**. Initially, this may sound like a weird argument, but it was pretty brilliant. Aquinas argued that it's clearly observable that everything in the universe that moves is moved by something else. The series of movements in the universe must have begun with a Prime Mover, which cannot be moved.

2) **The argument from causation**. A statue has a cause in the sculptor that carved it, but something else caused the sculptor to carve the statue. Whatever that cause was also had a prior cause. Every effect has a cause, but there cannot logically be an infinite chain of causes. Something must be the uncaused First Cause of change in the world.

3) **The argument from contingency**. I don't exist on my own. I am contingent on the air in our planet's atmosphere, but the earth doesn't exist on its own. It is contingent on the sun. The sun is contingent on the existence of gas and dust. On and on we

could go. All that is dependent on something else for its existence is not necessary. But not everything can be contingent. Something logically has to be necessary. That which is necessary for there to be anything at all is God.

4)   **The argument from perfection**. All things possess varying degrees of perfection of truth, goodness, or beauty. If you can imagine that something good could be even better, could you keep scaling up from better to better until you get to some superlative best that you cannot transcend? The highest truth, goodness, and beauty and the fount of it all, that we experience in diminished scale in creation is God.

5)   **The argument from design or order (sometimes known as the** *teleological argument***)**. Everything that exists has a purpose or goal for existing. We see things that would have no built-in intelligence acting in order toward their goal. If they cannot willingly move towards their ordered goal of their own accord, something must be directing them towards their proper ends. Like an "arrow is directed by the archer," God moves all natural things to their proper, ordered goal.

Now heavy, voluminous books have been written on Aquinas 'five proofs, so by no means does this short summary do it justice (if you're interested in reading more, follow this endnote to an excellent scholarly book on it [64]). Still, for many who have wrestled with the problem of evil, Aquinas 'arguments for the existence of God have kept them from atheism. This alone is not all that Aquinas had to contribute to discussions on the problem of evil. Because he attempted to give a theology of everything, we have many more insights from him to consider.

Aquinas continued the tradition of the Church's teaching on evil established by predecessors like Origen, Gregory of Nyssa, and most famously Augustine by claiming that evil was not so much a thing in and of itself, but evil was merely a privation of the Good. Because of Augustine's influence, this had become the default definition of evil through Christian theology in the West. While Plato influenced Origen, Gregory of Nyssa, and Augustine, a contemporary revival of interest in Plato's student Aristotle during Aquinas' lifetime played a major role in shaping what we now call Thomistic thought. While in Platonic philosophy, the material world was just a shadow or imperfect manifestation of the spiritual world, or the world of forms (this is called *idealism*), Aristotelian philosophy argued that reality actually is the observable, material world. It's not just an imperfect shadow. This is called *realism*.

This might help you make some sense of that famous painting of Plato and Aristotle by Raphael called *The School of Athens* (I've included it on this page). You might have noticed that Plato is pointing up while Aristotle is pointing down. That's because Plato believes what's *really* real is the spiritual world of forms above in the heavens, while Aristotle believes what's *really* real is the material world below.

It's important to understand that Aquinas primarily agrees with Aristotle, but not without a few tweaks and additions of his own. While Plato believed that if you looked at a chair, you recognized that material chair even with its imperfections because there was a perfect spiritual form of a chair that your soul could recognize, Aristotle thought this was unnecessary. We deduce what a chair is using our sense experiences, not our souls. Aquinas believes that things do exist in an immaterial form in our minds as intellectual knowledge, but get deduced truly through our sensory experiences. The mind develops a universal picture of what a chair looks like based on our sense experiences of the various chairs we've encountered so that when we see a brand new chair we've never encountered before, we can still recognize that it's a chair and not a giraffe based on the minds cataloging of past sensory experiences.

I almost have a sensory experience now of your mind going, "um, what does this have to do with the problem of evil?" But it's not some irrelevant detour. For Aquinas, this is central to believing that God's creation is actually good and not just a flawed shadow. By affirming that God made the world good and that it is not merely a shadow, God has also given us sense experiences of the world we can trust. This is the theological and philosophical foundation for the discipline of science.

Aquinas believes that it is because God made our material world good and has given us the ability to discern with both our senses and our faculties of reason the effects of God's works in the material world that Christians should hold to a high view of reason and general revelation. It's hard to overstate just how vital Aquinas 'work is to the future alleviation of so much human suffering through the increasing scientific and medicinal progress that comes about due to the influence of his views on God and the workings of the world.

If God really has made a world that is good and has given us the abilities to discern the way the world functions, then that sets a much better foundation for people to eventually figure out that before you go blaming "the aerial spirit escaping from the eyes of the sick man [which] strikes the healthy person standing near and looking at the sick" (a working theory for what caused the spread of the bubonic plague in the 14th century[65]) you should maybe consider not dumping your raw sewage on the streets- as was still the norm in places as "civilized" as London, England. [66] It would still take several hundred years for

Aquinas' ideas on reason and science to truly take root in Europe, but the seeds of the Scientific Revolution can be found in the theology and philosophy of Aquinas.

In this rather ambitious *theology of everything*, did Aquinas attempt to give any explanation for where evil came from? It wouldn't be much of a theology of everything if he didn't. By and large, Aquinas echoes earlier Christian thought on the possible reasons why evil exists at all, citing a variation on what we've called the *logical metaphysical necessity* of evil. If God were to create a perfect world without the potentiality for evil, there would be no difference between God and what God created, and God cannot create God. Given that God created a world with potential, evil and suffering are a logical necessity of that kind of world. To quote the philosopher and expert on Aquinas, Brian Davies, "God can't make lions and lambs without the lambs having something to worry about."[67] We mustn't assume that all suffering is inherently the result of evil. For Aquinas, we should make a distinction between two categories of evil.

The first category is what could be called *evil suffered*.[68] Many of the evils we may deem as "natural evils" like the lion eating the lamb, you or I catching a virus, or even a natural disaster like a hurricane are just a byproduct of how creation functions. God wills the ultimate good of the whole of creation, but if this creation is going to have any degree of potentiality, then He must allow for it to have instances where we would look at a sliver of the whole and say, "that's not good." God doesn't necessarily will directly that this kind of evil should happen in every instance. To put it another way- God is not the secondary cause of all this suffering. God is the primary cause in that He is the first cause of all things, and by His will, He holds all things that exist together, but that doesn't mean that God directly blows hurricanes towards the Gulf Coast just because He wills that a world where hurricanes can happen is a world still worth existing.

The second category of evil for Aquinas is what we

63

could call *evil done*.[69] These are the moral evils that rational beings misuse their will to perpetrate on others and the world around them. Moral evil is any act that goes against natural law, discernible by reason, and divine law, which is knowable through revelation. People need not have ever read a page of the Bible or heard the name of Jesus to be accountable for their actions because God has revealed so much of his will in the good, material world He created. All you need are your faculties of reason to pick up on the fact that doing something like murdering your neighbor just ain't right. Aquinas believes that's Romans 1 *101*. But if God made the world so good and all people of sound mind are able to use their faculties of reason to at least discern his laws in nature, then why do people still transgress his ways?

We shouldn't assume that just because Aquinas has a high view of the goodness of creation and general revelation that he did not take the effects of the fall seriously. For Aquinas, the fundamental issue behind the first sin of the primordial couple was that Adam and Eve misused their potentiality to be like God and confused it for a desire to be in God's role themselves.[70] They desired beyond the capacity of their God-given nature and were deceived by Satan in pursuing something they thought was a good but, in actuality, was a dis-ordering of God's functional design of the cosmos. Aquinas believed that this mistaken pursuit of something we wrongly perceive as a good was at the core of all *evil done*.

As a practical example, consider a married person who considers cheating on their spouse. What are they drawn to? Maybe pleasure, companionship, or affirmation. In and of themselves, none of these desires are wrong. The question is whether or not this is the rightly ordered path for actually pursuing those goods. For Aquinas, each person, when filled with an appetite or a desire for something they perceive to be good, should instantly check that desire against both reason and God's revelation contained in the Scriptures. If a person acts to attain the perceived good without checking to see if it is in keeping with God's will, they will inevitably inflict harm on others and themselves through their dysfunctional pursuit. In that way, there are "natural" painful consequences for those decisions, but even this pain is part of the right-ordering of God's love designed to deter us from continuing toward evil. Though God is the primary cause of all things, in that nothing exists apart from Him, Aquinas does not believe that God is the direct or secondary cause of our willful choices.

What is the highest and best good that the human will can reach for? For Aquinas, it is *caritas* or selfless love.[71] Caritas isn't something that the will just musters up, though. Caritas is received as a manifestation of God's love through the indwelling of the Holy Spirit. It is the highest and most noblest of all the virtues because it is the proper manifestation of what it means to act in keeping with our nature and end goal as creatures made in the image of God.

9. MARTIN LUTHER & JOHN CALVIN: DOES IT ALL COME FROM GOD?

While there were many reform movements throughout the Middle Ages aimed at trying to correct the perceived errors in theology, church politics, and morality of church leaders in the Roman Catholic Church, Martin Luther's famous posting of his Ninety-Five Theses on the doors of the church in Wittenberg in the year 1517 undoubtedly sparked the most revolutionary efforts at reform in church history. Luther was a devout Augustinian friar who initially thought that Pope Leo X must simply have no idea how corrupt the system of indulgences was and how much local bishops and priests were exploiting the poor people of places like Wittenberg.

Indulgences were deeply tied to the Catholic theology of *penance* which developed in the later years of the medieval church. Penance was one of the sacraments of the Catholic Church, that is, a means of grace by which God's spiritual grace could somehow be mediated to a person. This particular sacrament was set up in order to cover sins people committed after they had been baptized. So let's say that after you've been baptized, you steal a loaf of bread from the market. In order for that sin to be forgiven on judgment day, you need the grace to cover it.

The problem is that you've already received Christ's grace when you were baptized, so what are you going to do now that you're still sinning, you silly knucklehead? Well, you're going to need to confess that sin to someone the Church considers an authorized agent on God's behalf. So who can be that authorized agent? Can you go to your neighbor and just confess to him? Of course not! He's just a silly, sinful knucklehead too. What if that neighbor is a Christian though? Doesn't matter. You'll need to confess to an authorized agent that has been officially recognized by the institutional authority of the Roman Catholic Church...but confession might not be all that you have to do! You are still indebted to God's justice now and in order to have that debt satisfied the priest will recommend certain actions to limit your time in post-mortem purgatory where you will have to stay until you've paid off all of your sin debts.

If you're thinking, "But I've got a big sin debt!" Then there's good news. Well...sort of good news. You don't have to pay that debt alone. You can depend on something called the "Treasury of Merit" which contains a deposit of Christ's goodness and the goodness of dead saints from the past. If you want access to that account to pay your debt bill, the pope and the authority of the institutional Church can access that treasury for you. By the time Luther was on the scene, a complex system of paid-for indulgences has developed so that you don't have to just work off your debt to access the Treasury of Merit; you can just cut the Church a check.

So Luther's emphasis on "justification by grace through faith alone" has to be understood in light of this context. And if you can see how bad this is for a business bringing in bucks off indulgences, then you can understand why the Roman Catholic Church excommunicated him in 1521.

Usually, when people study Martin Luther, they are primarily focused on the events and theology that sparked the Reformation, but Luther's theology on sin, evil, suffering, and God's providence is profoundly influential on future generations of Protestants - even those that don't think of themselves as Lutheran at all. Luther was deeply influenced by the philosophy of William of Ockham. Maybe you've heard of Ockham's Razor before? That's the theory that when you have a bunch of competing theories or explanations for how something works, it's best to go with the simplest explanation first. This might be why you don't find in Luther's work complex metaphysical systems of philosophy or grandiose theologies of everything like you do with Thomas Aquinas.

So when it comes to the problem of evil, Luther doesn't give us a complex cosmology like Origen, nor does he give a comprehensive systematic theology like a subsequent reformer named John Calvin. Reading Luther and trying to figure out where he stands on evil and suffering can be confusing because he, frankly, isn't consistent all the time, at least in the way a rigorous systematic theologian attempts to be. This doesn't mean we're devoid of relevant contributions on the subject from Luther. It's quite the opposite.

For Luther, there is ultimately no rational way to solve the problem of why God allows evil. Instead, Luther gives some relevant core convictions. First, God is omnipotent, which means that God is ultimately responsible for everything, including evil and suffering. Second, the fall of Adam and Eve created natural evils in the world. Luther believed that before the fall of Adam and Eve (who Luther believes are not just archetypes but the first historical humans to have been created), everything on earth was in a state of perfection and free from all evil and suffering. There were no weeds or poison ivy in the garden, no tornadoes or tsunamis, and much to the delight of this author who lives in Minnesota, no mosquitoes.[72] Because of Adam and Eve's sin, the world now has weeds, illnesses, hurricanes, and even those stupid mosquitoes. This was not a brand new idea. In fact, it was fairly in keeping with the Augustinian perspective on the cause of natural evils.

The third core conviction of Luther that's relative to our journey on the problem of evil is his view on the nature of God's omnipotence. Because God is omnipotent, nothing happens apart from his will. Even the choices that we perceive as being born from our own free will are not freely ours to have chosen. "You [God] exalt us when you humble us. You make us righteous when you make us sinners. You lead us to heaven when you cast us into hell. You grant us the victory when you cause us to be defeated. You give life when you permit us to be killed." [73]

In Luther's theodicy, we can see a return to the sort of monistic theodicy one might find in ancient Judaism. God gives and God takes away. Often the sufferings we experience as something terrible to be avoided are nothing more than the *opus alienum Dei*, or the "alien works of God."[74] The alien works of God that make us feel a sense of terror are necessary in order for us to experience the *opus proprium Dei*, or the proper works of God, such as mercy and forgiveness. The Cross is the ultimate example of the harmony between the alien acts of God and the proper works of God, as God's mercy and forgiveness are revealed most clearly as the Son experiences the most pain, shame, and abandonment on the Cross. Life may be brutal and full of pain, but God himself has experienced this in Christ. This is a difficult paradox that Luther believed can't be solved by reason but by faith. Luther believed that God is both the source of all life and, as Charlene Burns puts it, "the destructive power of the cosmos that seems indifferent to us."[75]

For Luther, we should spend less time worrying about the metaphysics and philosophy of all this and more time focused on the appropriate response to God in the face of suffering. For Luther, the best response, whether we experience good or bad, joy or pain, is to turn to God because "everything is sent by God, whether it comes from devil or man." [76] This doesn't mean that we completely ignore Satan or reject that he exists. Luther talks about Satan quite a bit.

> "It was not a unique, unheard of thing for the Devil
> to hump about and haunt houses. In our monastery
> at Wittenberg I hear him distinctly...the Devil came
> and thudded three times in the storage chamber...

also I heard him once over my chamber...but when I realized it was Satan, I rolled over and went back to sleep again."[77]

Because Luther believed so strongly in the omnipotent, determining providence of God, he also feels assured that Satan is nothing more than a barking dog on God's leash. He can bark, but he ain't got no bite.

One of Luther's most vocal critics for his views on the nature of God's omnipotence, human free will, and much more was a Dutch philosopher and theologian named Desiderius Erasmus. Erasmus had written a book entitled *The Free Will* as part of his own efforts to reform the immorality he perceived in the Catholic Church through a call to ethical living. Luther fired back at Erasmus 'concept of free will in a treatise entitled *The Bondage of the Will*. In it, Luther argued that the human will was simply a beast caught between two riders. One rider is God, and the other rider is Satan. Free will was just a "name without a reality."[78]

Erasmus believed that God had foreknowledge of all things, including our choices, but that this foreknowledge did not mean that our choices were predestined. After all, why would God even give commands if we could not follow them? Luther argued that was the point. We had no ability to follow the Law and were completely and utterly dependent on the grace of God. God is God and doesn't need to be defended from our accusations of being unjust. God isn't looking for lawyers to defend Him; He's looking for people to trust Him.

In this way, Luther sees himself as recovering the true Augustinian tradition that the Church had lost sight of. In keeping with the later writings of Augustine, Luther even believes that the damnation of the lost is simply part of the incomprehensible will of God.

"God hardens the will of man so that he desires to transgress the divine Law all the more. Hence, God is the cause of why men sin and are condemned. This is the strongest and most weighty objection. But the Apostle meets it by saying that so it is God's will, and that if God so wills He does not act unjustly, for all things belong to Him as the clay belongs to the potter. He thus establishes His law in order that the elect may obey it, but the reprobates may be caught in it, and so He may show both His wrath and His mercy."[79]

This view, called *double predestination*, is often attributed to John Calvin, but one can see in Luther's theology a precedent of attempting to connect this doctrine to Augustine, who both Luther and Calvin viewed as the early church's most authoritative interpreter of Scripture. Now double predestination is not a view held by most Lutherans today, primarily because Luther was not a systematic theologian who continued to return to systematic arguments about this point throughout his career. Many modern Lutherans may prefer to think of God's predestination of the elect as a "single predestination" whereby God has merely predestined those who will receive salvation. Many a seminary lunch table has been filled with debates about whether there is any meaningful distinction between the two positions.

Is there a difference between foreknowledge and foreordination? If God perfectly foreknew that Judas would betray Jesus, could Judas really have done other than what God perfectly foreknew he would do? Luther didn't believe that Judas could do otherwise because Judas 'will was bound to Satan as its rider. This brings up all sorts of challenging questions about whether or not we should consider Judas or any other sinner morally responsible for their sin. Erasmus thought it was ridiculous for God to hold people responsible for their sins if they weren't free to do anything other than sin. This undid any value in ethical instruction and gave people an excuse for their sins. Luther preferred not even to try and solve the apparent logical incongruities, and maintained that the special revelation of Scripture demonstrates that God is both sovereign and good. We should merely have faith in his sovereignty and goodness.

$$* * *$$

John Calvin was born 26 years after Luther and is considered part of the next generation of Protestant Reformers. He was a brilliant mind and much more interested in systematic theology than Luther was. Calvin was a trained lawyer, and you can see evidence of that in how he wrote his theology. The most famous of all his writings was a massive systematic theology entitled *Institutes of the Christian Religion*. While Calvin was far more logical and systematic in his writings, he did not veer far from Luther's theology, including Luther's views on evil, suffering, human will, and salvation. Like Luther, Calvin didn't see himself as breaking away to start a new denomination or church. He wanted the Church to return to its earliest sources to help guide the interpretation of Scripture. As New Testament scholar Matthew J. Thomas highlights in his *Paul's "Works of the Law" in the Perspective of Second-Century Reception*, Luther and Calvin more than likely did not have access to the same level of early church writings as we do today, but what they did have access to was Augustine.[80]

Calvin agreed with Luther on his concepts of the hiddenness of God and the alien acts of God. He agreed that the Devil was real but was employed by God to "instigate the reprobate."[81] What Luther seems to imply about double predestination, Calvin makes more explicit:

> "By predestination we mean the eternal decree of God, by which he determined with himself whatever he wished to happen with regard to every man. All are not created on equal terms, but some are preordained to eternal life [election], others to

eternal damnation [reprobation]."[82]

God decreed before the foundations of the world who would be saved and who would be damned. Calvin was aware of how off-putting that sounds to most people's sensibilities, but if this is what Scripture teaches (and Calvin is convinced that this is the teaching of Paul in the New Testament), then we must adjust our views accordingly. Not only that, but if one believes the same metaphysical claims that Augustine and Aquinas both made about the nature of God and His omniscience, immutability, and existence beyond time itself, then logically, all of history is a settled fact to the mind of God. Not only that, but if God is omnipotent, then it is also logically necessary that this history is happening just as He planned for it to go. If it isn't, then are we suggesting that some force greater than God is making history go in a way God did not want or planned?

Should any of this knowledge diminish our desire to care for the world and the people around us? Calvin answers with a resounding no. We have no idea who the elect and the reprobate are, so we must act as if everyone we encounter is possibly part of the elect pre-appointed by God to receive salvation.

Augustine had Pelagius, Luther had Erasmus, and Calvin had his own rival named Jacob Arminius. The only difference is that Arminius and Calvin never met. Arminius was only four years old when Calvin died. So when boys and girls stay up late in their Christian college dorm rooms debating Calvinism vs. Arminianism, they are actually arguing about a debate between the next generation of Calvinists and Jacob Arminius and his followers. Arminius believed that Calvin's doctrine of predestination and "limited" atonement made God evil and the Scriptures completely nonsensical. Arminius wasn't arguing anything new, just like Calvin wasn't arguing anything new. Still, Christians in various denominations of the Protestant tradition often like to frame questions about God's sovereignty, free will, and predestination as "Calvinism vs. Arminianism," even though you can trace both men's theologies to far earlier sources.

Historically in the Protestant tradition, Charismatics, Pentecostals, Wesleyans, Methodists, Anabaptists, and other "general" baptists have rejected Calvin's views on these matters, while Presbyterians, Reformed churches like the Dutch Reformed or Christian Reformed Church, and Reformed and Calvinist Baptists have sided with Calvin's views on predestination and salvation. Lutherans largely tried to stay out of the whole debate even though Luther had more in common with Calvin's theology than Arminius 'theology.

If you began this book having come from any of these particular Protestant denominations, chances are you already had some conclusions about Luther or Calvin's theology. That's completely understandable. My goal in walking you through their theologies is to allow you to compare, contrast, and evaluate them. I'm sincerely not trying to talk you into agreeing or disagreeing with them. What's more important to this journey is hopefully helping you see that whether you liked them or not, their positions were not completely unreasonable and are shared by millions of your Christian brothers and sisters around the globe.

It was not entirely unreasonable for Calvin to suggest that when talking about God's will and foreknowledge, these prior complex categories like "absolute necessity" or "conditional necessity" don't seem to have an obvious line of distinction. If what God eternally foreknows is going to happen regardless, where is the line of distinction? Does it really matter whether you want to call that "eternally foreknowing" or "eternally causing"? As harsh as Calvin may appear to some of you, perhaps he's just willing to be more brutally honest about what he thinks is a negligible difference between foreknowledge and predestination. The question he would pose back to those who may have a problem with his perspective might be, "Okay, you disagree..so explain to me how free will can exist if God is omniscient. Won't you always do what God knows you will do? And if you can't do otherwise, are you free?"

Whatever you make of Calvin's arguments, they were so strong that they almost instantly provoked creative responses from those who thought that some other explanation must be able to work in order to preserve the goodness of God and human free will. Some of these attempts in the years to come began to wildly break away from what we could now call "classical theism" in an effort to address issues with the problem of evil and suffering that many still found unresolved after 1600 years of Christian thought.

PART III- COMPARING HISTORICAL PERSPECTIVES:

MODERN PERSPECTIVES

10. MOLINISM: IS THIS THE BEST POSSIBLE WORLD?

Remember that scene in *Avengers: Infinity War* when Dr. Strange uses the time stone to browse through 14,000,605 possible futures in order to determine what it will take for the Avengers to defeat Thanos, and he finds only one possible world where Thanos loses? What if God's foreknowledge was something like that? Obviously, in the 16th century, theologians and philosophers weren't thinking about Marvel movies, but there were some who were considering creative alternatives to the classical notions of divine foreknowledge and omniscience that might sound to us like something from a big box office superhero movie. The Catholic Church had long struggled with how to reconcile together two core beliefs. How can God's grace be the supreme cause of salvation and not human will, as Augustine taught, and how can the human will also be totally free and responsible for its consent or rejection of God's grace?

Most Catholics were just as upset with Calvinism as the Arminians were. If the human will is not free and God has predestined all things, then how can God not be responsible for all evil, suffering, and the involuntary damnation of much of the human race? The 18th-century free-will theologian John Wesley summed up the general opposition to "predestinarianism" well when he wrote, "You represent God as worse than the devil;

more false, more cruel, more unjust. But you say you will prove it by Scripture. Hold! What will you prove by Scripture? That God is worse than the devil? It cannot be. Whatever that Scripture proves, it never proved this; whatever its true meaning be, this cannot be its true meaning."[83] The problem for those that opposed Calvin was that he made such a strong case within the assumptions of classical theism that perhaps the only way to counter his arguments effectively was to challenge some of the long-held presuppositions in classical theism. One of the first to creatively attempt this was a 16th-century Spanish priest named Luis de Molina.

Molina tried to come up with a way of explaining the mysterious interaction between God's will and human will in such a way that it would neither infer that God is the cause of evil nor make the case that the human will was the cause of its own salvation. To do this, he made a creative tweak to the metaphysics of classical theism and challenged some of the traditional views on God. In the classical view, God perfectly and eternally foresees all human actions in a singular timeline that originates and ends in God's divine decree. If you remember Luther and Erasmus 'argument, you'll remember that there have always been some who didn't see God's eternal foreknowledge and human free will as irreconcilable. But philosophical efforts to explain how this could be so were always debated. Molina tried to come up with a workaround.

What if, logically prior to God's decree to create the cosmos, God had knowledge not only of everything that moral agents *could* do but also everything that they *would* do in any possible scenario? Molina called this kind of knowledge *middle knowledge*. Using middle knowledge, God is able to see what would have happened if a person was put in a particular situation. These are called *counterfactuals*. Again (and this is a crude analogy), picture Dr. Strange mentally scrolling through all of the possible scenarios that could defeat Thanos to find the best one. In a sense, God could run countless simulations of the billions of people who could ever live and the innumerable situations those people could experience to see how they would freely respond in each situation. Based on this middle knowledge, God then actualizes the best possible world that fulfills his purposes through the free choices of moral agents.

Maybe another movie analogy might be helpful to better understand this concept of middle knowledge. Picture the fictional story of George Bailey (played by Jimmy Stewart) in the holiday classic *It's a Wonderful Life*. You could say that God gave George middle knowledge of a world that was far worse off without him. Even though the actual world was still filled with suffering and disappointment for George, he eventually sees that the actual world was better than this other possible world even if that meant he could end up bankrupt and in jail. Of course, *It's a Wonderful Life* has a happy ending with this beautiful redemptive moment where all of the difficulties of George's life get resolved. Surrounded by his wife, kids, and community of friends who love him, nearly the entire town shows up to put their money back in his bank so that he won't go bankrupt and end up in jail. They gather together in his home, with the final resolution being a joyful chorus of Auld Lang Syne.

If we interpret this movie through a Molinist lens, we can see how Molinism attempts to address the problem of evil and suffering. God, in His sovereignty, has decided it is good for a world to exist containing rational creatures with the capacity to choose. As a creative offshoot of the Augustinian tradition, Molinism teaches that God cannot make a world that is without any deficiency in truth, goodness, or beauty because to do so would mean that God could create another God. This is a logical impossibility. The world (and by this, I mean not just planet earth but all contingent reality) contains potentiality and possibility. This means that it is possible for the world to move away from the Good. So God runs innumerable mental "simulations" of possible worlds with moral agents, both human and angelic, who have libertarian free will. Trillions upon trillions of *It's a Wonderful Life* scenarios, a truly innumerable & humanly incalculable set of possible worlds processed and analyzed with God selecting the best of them all.

Granted, a proper Molinist will tell you that all of these analogies fail, primarily because, as beings trapped within time, we can't help but imagine God's middle knowledge as if God were somehow in time processing through a list of possible worlds. Molina would tell you that God didn't take time to calculate the best possible world. Not to make matters more confusing, but God's usage of middle knowledge to actualize the best possible world is *logically* prior not *temporally* prior. It's okay to be confused at this point.

Another analogy that the contemporary Molinist philosopher William Lane Craig uses to try and explain Molinism is that of God being dealt a hand of cards. In one sense, Craig acknowledges in this analogy that limitations have been placed on God for how this game of cards will go because God has turned the deck over to be shuffled by the free will of moral agents. Despite the horrific things moral agents can do with their will, God plays his cards "skilfully" and "in such a way that his ultimate ends are achieved through creaturely free decisions, despite the sinful decisions they would make and the evils they would bring about."[84] Craig goes on to write:

> "God's absolute intentions are thus often frustrated by sinful creatures, but his conditional intentions, which take into account creatures 'free actions, are always fulfilled...Even sin serves God's conditional intentions in that it manifests his overflowing goodness in the incarnation of Christ for the purpose of rescuing humanity from sin, his power in his redeeming humanity from sin, and his justice in punishing sin."[85]

There are many tragic and horrific evils that seem utterly senseless to us, but the Molinist response to those evils is to remind us that while these evils may seem senseless to us, it is because we do not possess God's omniscience and cannot see how something as horrific as the death of a child or a tragic terrorist attack will have a positive ripple effect that leads to an ultimately redemptive, good, and beautiful end to the story of history. The modern Molinist might point you to the "butterfly effect" as an example of the human limitations in understanding cause and effect. The butterfly effect is a principle coined by the award-winning mathematician and meteorologist Edward Lorenz. He demonstrated that something as small and seemingly insignificant as a butterfly flapping its wings in Southeast Asia could be a determining factor in the formation of a tornado that hits Oklahoma weeks later. For the Molinist, even what seems like the most senseless evil or suffering isn't senseless. Perhaps it is the unfortunate but necessary flap of a butterfly's wings that God foreknew and permitted in order to bring about the best possible ending for the whole of creation.

Returning to our Hollywood movie comparisons, one could ask whether or not it was a morally sufficient reason for Dr. Strange to allow Tony Stark/IronMan to die a painful death to stop a far worse evil. In the same way, the Molinist would argue that we must trust the omniscient wisdom of God and His omnibenevolent goodness that He has morally sufficient reasons for why everything from the Holocaust to the seemingly senseless death of a loved one in a car accident involving a drunk driver has been allowed. These acts of evil and suffering are not good, but the Molinist believes that in the end, when the story has reached its happy conclusion, we will see that the actual world God brought to be was the best possible world.

Whether you consider Molinism a viable option for answering your questions about the problem of evil and suffering or whether you think it's confusing rubbish, Molinism never quite garnered the same level of prominence in Christian theology as the Augustinian, Thomistic, Lutheran, or Calvinist traditions. Some Catholics, especially in the Dominican order, accused him of heresy. After decades of debate, Pope Paul V declared in 1607 that there should be no more accusations of heresy against the Molinists. Roman Catholics were free to hold to the classical or Molinist positions.[86]

But what were the strongest objections to Molinism? For both classical theists in the Roman Catholic church and those who followed the Lutheran or Reformed perspectives, there were shared concerns that Molina gave too much power to the wills of human and angelic moral agents. If God is limited to play the hand that He's dealt by our free will, then who is really the God in this relationship? As contemporary theologian Philip Carey responded to William Lane Craig's deck of cards analogy, "The cards limit God's options, for they imply that not every possible world is one God could feasibly actualize."[87] If God is answering to powers beyond his final say, then sure it makes for a more straightforward explanation of why there is evil and suffering, but then you are left with God being functionally a demigod still answering to a higher power in the hierarchy of cosmic command. If that is the case, we should name that higher power "God." The classical objection is that Molinism makes *human will* God.

Another challenge for Molinism put forward by classical theists and open theists (who we will explore in chapter 15) is that, presumably, God saw the world with the Holocaust and Hiroshima as the best possible world. Given that this is the world God chose to bring about and that this is the only actual world, wasn't someone like Hitler still bound to turn out evil? God knew that Hitler would respond to the harsh punishments on Germany from the Treaty of Versaille at the end of World War I with the vengeful fire to bring Germany back to global power. God knew that Hitler would lead a racist, genocidal crusade against the Jewish people, and knowing full well that Hitler would respond that way, God created this one actual world where Hitler commits these terrible atrocities. Was there a possible world where Hitler is presented with a different set of circumstances that lead him to become a humanitarian? Or maybe there was another possible world where Hitler's parents never conceived a child. If that is true, then to what degree is Hitler responsible for his actions?

The cards that God has been dealt and Hitler have been dealt seem like a problem not only for Hitler but for the six million Jews who died under his ruthless regime. Wouldn't any of us, if put in the wrong situation at the wrong time, possibly become horrible moral monsters?

This is the premise of Alan Moore's 1988 comic *The Killing Joke,* which tells one possible story of how Joker becomes a sadistic murdering clown in Batman's Gotham City. In the story, an unnamed man goes through a series of tragedies, many of which seem outside his control. Through these series of tragedies, including the tragic death of his pregnant wife and dangerous gangsters forcing his participation in a crime at an old chemical plant he used to be an engineer at, the man eventually comes face to face with Batman. Out of utter fear, he jumps into the hazardous chemicals and emerges with bleached skin, green hair, and clown-like red lips. The sheer sight of his disfigurement becomes the last straw that causes him to snap. Throughout the rest of the comic, he goes on a horrific rampage. In the penultimate confrontation with Batman, Joker says to the caped crusader:

> "All it takes is one bad day to reduce the sanest man alive to lunacy. That's how far the world is from where I am. Just one bad day. You had a bad day once. Am I right? I know I am. I can tell. You had a bad day and everything changed."[88]

If Molinism is true, should we look upon the Jokers of the world with sympathy? And what would we make of this Molinist theodicy if it is also paired with the idea that Hitler will endure eternal conscious torment for crimes that he inevitably had to commit in this one actual world? Some, still unsatisfied with the answers of Molina or any of his predecessors, will wonder whether we place too much emphasis on special revelation and instead should look more towards the light of general revelation in the natural world in order to better understand God's nature and character.

11. GOTTFRIED LEIBNIZ: NATURAL THEOLOGY & THE BEST OF ALL POSSIBLE WORLDS

By the 17th and into the 18th century, many of the inhabitants of Europe and North America were growing tired of the God of Christendom. Well past the horrors of the Crusades and the Spanish Inquisition, post-Reformation Europe had many horrific incidents of suffering induced by those who claim to be Christian. Throughout Europe, and quite infamously in Salem, Massachusetts, you had witch trials during the 17th century. During that period, as many as 100,000 people were executed for witchcraft, 80,000 of which were women. These weren't isolated to either Catholic lands or Protestant lands. It happened in both areas, with the worst incidents in Catholic German lands and in Calvinist regions of Scotland.[89] All this, combined with various religious wars, created a burgeoning response of cynicism and distrust for Christianity- a response that we still feel to this very day.

Running parallel with the growing distrust of institutionalized Christian religion was a developing scientific revolution, birthed in no small part because of Aquinas' theological affirmation of reason and general revelation centuries before. Many of these scientific discoveries shattered our prior understandings of the world. The realization that the earth is not the center of the universe called into question the centrality of our place in the cosmos. If what appeared so obvious as we looked outside was wrong (just look outside and watch the sun move across the sky throughout the day and tell me that people weren't crazy for thinking that the sun revolved around the earth), what else could we be wrong about?

Newton's laws of physics pointed to a universe that functioned like a giant machine, automated by a designer to run without the need for direct control by God. Discoveries like this began to call into question long-held theologies. This revolution in science and math led to the rise of rationalism and natural theology as the West moved into a period historians commonly refer to as "the Enlightenment."

Natural theology puts a primary emphasis on the role of reason in understanding God and His world. We could deduce the truth about God by observing His laws that we see governing nature. One of the best examples of a natural theologian was the 17th-century mathematician and philosopher Gottfried Leibniz.

Leibniz was possibly one of the most brilliant human beings to ever live. He developed calculus, the first mechanical calculator, and some have even argued that he was the founder of artificial intelligence....in the 17th century![90] Leibniz considered himself a Christian but placed a primary emphasis on the role of reason in discerning truth. There are many natural theologians we could point to during this time, but Leibniz is arguably the most significant natural theologian of his era to seriously address the problem of evil. In fact, as I mentioned in this book's introduction, it was Leibniz who coined the term *theodicy*.

When he wasn't inventing calculus, the binary numeric coding system fundamental to computer language, or attempting to design artificial intelligence, he was writing about God, the problem of evil, and some of life's most perplexing questions. His most important project on this subject was his 1710 work entitled *Theodicy: Essays on the Goodness of God, the Freedom of Man, and the Origin of Evil*. Leibniz wrote this book because he was so upset by the argument of a French Huguenot named Pierre Bayle. Bayle had argued that there was simply no rational way to solve the problem of evil without making God responsible for the world's evils.[91]

Leibniz rejected some of the other more controversial opinions on the problem of evil in his day, including a precursor to Open Theism called *Socinianism* which held to the belief that there were contingent truths that God did not know (because if God were to know all things than free will becomes a logical impossibility).[92] Leibniz did not think this had to be the case and attempted, using reason over biblical exegesis, to defend more classical conceptions of God- specifically, that God is both perfectly good and completely omnipotent.

Like previous scholastic philosophers, Leibniz argued that all effects logically require a prior cause. The problem is that you can't just have an infinite regress of causes without a fundamental uncaused cause. Echoing other classical predecessors, Leibniz also argued that for this Uncaused Causer to be the perfection of truth, goodness, and beauty, what God created could not simultaneously be perfect in truth, goodness, or beauty. The contingent creation has to be different from the necessary creator. This creates the first category of evil, which we have already called *metaphysical evil*.[93]

Any possible world must have some deficiency in it in comparison to God. Like Molina, Leibniz believed that there could have been a nearly infinite range of possible worlds God could have created, but because God is the infinite fount of wisdom, the world that God brought into existence was the best possible world. Yes, there is evil and suffering, but Leibniz believed that the sum total of goodness in creation vastly outweighs the evil and suffering. Leibniz even thought it was a statistical probability that life exists on other planets throughout the universe, and that when that is taken into account, the natural and moral evils we experience are utterly dwarfed by the total weight of the goodness of creation. That is not to say that everything that happens right now should be celebrated as good. God's intended trajectory for creation is not yet complete. When that day comes, we will see that every instance of temporary pain or suffering was worth God bringing this world to bear. [94]

Our biggest problem is that we can't see the whole picture and don't have the computational power in our brains to do the math and realize how minuscule the evil is in comparison to the good. That doesn't mean Leibniz believes that God individually wills human moral evils (the second category of evil we find in Leibniz's writings). God allows freedom of the will as part of his wise decision to bring about the best possible world. Human souls are genuinely free.

The third category of evil for Leibniz is another familiar category to us thus far. Natural evil, according to Leibniz, is a byproduct of metaphysical evil. Leibniz argues that the tiny building blocks of the universe, what he calls *monads*, have a degree of their own will and autonomy.[95] Though this would be an anachronistic expression on our part, we could say that Leibniz believes that everything has consciousness. The proper philosophical term for that idea today is *panpsychism*. This means that by God allowing a certain degree of free will to everything in the universe, it is possible for nature to even use its potentiality in ways that are not good. Destructive hurricanes and viruses are possible, not because God is directly (or secondarily) causing them to happen, but because God chose to make a world where these features are possible while knowing that it is still the best of all possible worlds.

Not everyone was wild with this sort of theodicy during the Enlightenment. Famously, the French Enlightenment author Voltaire wrote a fierce satirical takedown of this type of "best possible world" theodicy that we find in Molinism and

Leibniz's theology. In 1755, on All Saints Day, an earthquake rocked Lisbon, Portugal, killing approximately 60,000 people. Many, if not most, of these people were likely in church worshiping on All Saints Day. Voltaire wrote a satirical story in response about a fictional young man named Candide who runs into a seemingly endless thread of trouble. One of Candide's friends is a man named Dr. Pangloss. Pangloss is clearly a spoof on Leibniz and is a professor of "metaphysico-theologico-cosmo-nigology". There are a lot of big philosophical words in this book, but I promise you *that one* was made up by Voltaire as a joke. Dr. Pangloss satirically resembles Leibniz's theodicy when he says:

> "Things cannot be otherwise than as they are; for all being created for an end, all is necessarily for the best end. Observe that the nose has been formed to bear spectacles- thus we have spectacles. Legs are visibly designed for stockings- and we have stockings...Pigs were made to be eaten- therefore we eat pork all the year round. Consequently...all is for the best."[96]

After Candide experiences a string of misfortunes, he bumps into Dr. Pangloss again. This time Pangloss is a hideous beggar dying of syphilis. When Candide suggests that all of the evil and suffering they've endured must be from the Devil, Pangloss dismisses the notion and waxes philosophically about how what we perceive as evil are just the necessary ingredients in the best of all possible worlds. After all, if Columbus hadn't invaded the Americas and caught this disease that now spreads across the globe, Europeans wouldn't have had access to so much good chocolate.[97]

Defenders of the best of all possible worlds theodicy would argue that Voltaire missed the point and that Leibniz was never celebrating any singular moment of evil as good. But did Voltaire have a valid point? Would accepting a Leibniz-style theodicy eventually lead someone to a fatalistic apathy about the evils of the world? When should one respond to the evils and suffering of the world with a sense of rebellion because they know that evils are wrong?

Leibniz was one voice among many during this time championing the virtues of natural theology and rationalism, but as this rationalism eventually led to Deism, new theological voices emerged who challenged the supremacy of reason in discerning what God was like. In the next chapter, we'll explore a couple of those dissenting voices.

12. KANT & SCHLEIERMACHER: THE LIMITS OF REASON

During the Enlightenment, there was a growing movement of people that despised the Christian religion of the past. Philosophers like Voltaire and David Hume wrote as the precursors to our modern New Atheism of the 20-21st century. Like Richard Dawkins in our generation, David Hume's critiques of religion provoked many Christians to creatively respond to his objections. Immanuel Kant (1724-1804) read the work of Hume and said that Hume woke him from his "dogmatic slumber."[98]

Kant's parents were Lutheran Pietists, an often neglected feature of Kant's theological and philosophical formation. Pietism began in Germany as a movement hoping to return to "apostolic simplicity."[99] Pietists emphasized religious zeal, personal devotion, and relatively new ideas like small group Bible study without the aid of a priest. In many ways, the Pietist movement was the precursor to Evangelicalism. Pietism placed a heavy emphasis on faith and the subjective. Pietists believed that natural theologians placed too strong of an emphasis on the use of reason and general revelation. What was really needed was a revival of the primacy of special revelation.

During the 18th century, the West was having a spirited debate about the best method for how we can come to know the truth. One camp believed, like Leibniz, that reality is known through reason alone. They were called *rationalists*. The other camp believed that sense experience is the only way to know the truth. They were called *empiricists*. Immanuel Kant tried to figure out a third alternative and concluded that true knowledge does come from experience but our minds have pre-existing file folders that filter and organize those experiences. We never just experience things as they are. We experience them in the ways our brains can categorize them.

Maybe this gets you thinking back to the debate between Plato and Aristotle on whether we truly know things in the material world as they are or if we only see a shadow of their higher, spiritual forms. Kant doesn't deny that there is a spiritual or *noumenal realm*, but he believes that the best we can do is hypothesize about that realm because we only have access to the physical or *phenomenal world*...and even our access to that realm is never an unfiltered, purely objective experience! Our minds act as an interpretive file folder system that helps us make coherent sense of the phenomenal world.

For example, is time real? Could we somehow objectively prove, apart from our subjective experiences, that time is a thing that exists apart from us? Kant would say no. What we call time is a category of experience that our mind has a specific folder or app for that helps us make sense of our experience of the world (I'm using words like "file folder" or "app" but Kant obviously never uses those words). Kant's perspective has become known as *transcendental idealism*.[100]

Once again, this isn't some random detour we're taking into non-relevant philosophy. Having a basic grasp of Kant's transcendental idealism is vital for understanding how he and many others attempt to make sense of God, evil, and suffering even if they don't think of themselves as Kantians. Kant believed that because God exists in the noumenal realm or the absolute spiritual domain, and because knowledge of that domain exists beyond the boundaries of reason, much of our debate about metaphysics and theology just can't be reduced to rational arguments or empirical knowledge.

Take Job as one example. Job was about as righteous as a person can get, and yet there doesn't appear to be any rational connection between Job's virtuous living and a positive reward mechanism for that virtue. Job leads a good, virtuous life but experiences the worst evil and suffering imaginable. The teacher of Ecclesiastes seems to feel that there is no coherent rational connection between moral living and the reward of happiness or well-being. But for Kant, because God's existence and governance take place in the noumenal realm beyond the bounds of reason and sense experience, it should not surprise us that there isn't a rational, coherent principle that connects virtuous living to positive outcomes. If ethics, which come from God in the noumenal realm, are beyond the limits of reason, then we shouldn't presume to understand what the full consequence of virtuous living or sinful evil should do in the world. Even if we could figure this out, "hope for reward and fear of punishment would take the place of moral motives."[101]

For Kant, this whole business of trying to defend God against the evils and sufferings of our world is just plain foolishness. It's beyond our capabilities of reason. What if what we think of as "evil" are just things that run contrary to our sense of happiness? How could we know whether or not those experiences aren't just because of some larger good purpose of God? Suppose one argues that this could be the case, but that genuine evil still exists and should be thought of as events that run contrary to God's purposes. How are we supposed to be able to tell the difference from our infinitesimally small vantage point? Kant believed there could never be a theodicy that completely removes all doubt about God. So the answer to the problem of evil isn't rational or empirical knowledge. It's faith.

Kant believed that reason and faith weren't at odds but were instead like concentric circles with reason as the inner circle and supra-rational religious experience as the outer circle.

Reason, in the inner circle, can help us deduce the existence of an outer circle. In fact, the inner circle depends on the existence of the outer circle. We can use faculties of reason to deduce that killing your neighbor is immoral, but we need an ultimate Law-Giver to create morality in the first place.[102]

***

Freidrich Schleiermacher (1768-1834) was a German theology professor and an ordained minister in the Reformed Church who agreed with Kant on the limitations of reason. In an era when it was becoming increasingly en vogue to denounce religion, Schleiermacher saw himself as defending Christian belief from the "cultured despisers" of his day. [103] In doing so, he attempted to redefine what Christianity could be for the modern person of his day. Schleiermacher does this by inverting the way Christian theology was typically done. He thought that instead of starting with the Bible or a list of acceptable doctrines, people should start with human experience and then see what doctrines fit within human experience. What fits should be preserved, and what doesn't should be set aside or reinterpreted.

Schleiermacher was raised in the Pietist tradition just like Immanuel Kant. That tradition emphasized the limits of human reasoning while highlighting the necessity of special revelation and the Spirit's work through the Bible as the beginning of knowledge, but Schleiermacher took that Pietist emphasis to a whole different level by suggesting that human experience, more specifically *feeling*, was the foundation for knowledge of God. Feeling was the bridge between the phenomenal world of reason and sense experience and the spiritual, noumenal world. We shouldn't expect the physical, phenomenal world to give us a complete picture of God. True religion is the "feeling of absolute dependence" on God, and that means that even instances of suffering we cannot understand rationally give us opportunities to place our dependence on Him.[104]

True evil is that which separates us from our dependence on God, or what Schleiermacher called *God-consciousness*. Evil presents itself to us as an opportunity to focus on life's obstacles instead of giving ourselves to God. But even these temptations to be distracted by life's obstacles don't have some independent source outside of God. Schleiermacher is no Gnostic. In fact, he believes that both good and evil are interdependent features rooted in God. There is no knowledge of what is good without evil. In this way, Schleiermacher doesn't believe that natural evils are genuinely evil. They only become evil when humans respond to them in a self-centered way that would disrupt our feeling of dependence on God.[105] Sin is what would keep us from absolute dependence on God, but even sin is not actually in opposition to God as God has other purposes even for our sin. Schleiermacher writes that God is "the Author of sin- of sin, however only as related to redemption."[106]

As troublesome as that may sound to many of you, Schleiermacher is trying to avoid the old Gnostic hyper-dualism at all costs. After all, if sin does not ultimately originate from the will of God, then what other point of origin does it come from? Beginning what would long be a hallmark of liberal theology after him, Schleiermacher also believed that Christianity should do away with the idea of Satan. In his mind, there were just too many problems with the idea. Why would angelic beings close to God ever willingly turn away? Who or what would have tempted Satan? Wouldn't there need to be some other pre-existent force of evil to tempt him?

According to Schleiermacher, blaming humanity's fall on Satan has never been helpful. We still need an explanation for the fall of Satan and who tempted the Tempter. Schleiermacher even believed that the whole idea of Satan undermined the importance of Jesus. Is there no Christ without there being a Satan? Was Jesus just a *plan B* because Satan and humanity rebelled? As unorthodox as Schleiermacher's theology is on this subject, he undoubtedly presents thought-provoking questions.

You can see in Kant and Schleiermacher the influence of Luther and his focus on how we should respond in faith to experiences of evil and suffering instead of trying to intellectually solve the problem of evil. Though most Evangelicals today would reject much of Kant and Schleiermacher's theology, the influence of their emphasis on the separation of reason and faith as one offshoot of Pietist theology is a prominent feature of the theology of many Evangelicals and other Protestants.

As you reflect on the ideas of Kant and Schleiermacher, I invite you to pause and consider where else you have possibly heard similar ideas from Christians about the limits of reason and the supremacy of knowing God's will through subjective experiences like "feeling"? What are the strengths and weaknesses of this approach?

13. DINOSAURS, DARWIN, & THE DEATH OF GOD

One of the common answers many Christians have historically given for why there are natural evils such as sickness or even animal suffering has been to blame Adam and Eve and their first sin as the event that ruptured the perfect ordering of creation. Especially among those influenced by the Augustinian tradition, there has been this understanding of the biblical story that begins with a perfect, utopian Garden of Eden free of any suffering or death. This utopian paradise is lost because of the first sin of the first humans- an event commonly known as *the Fall*. From that point onward, lions ate lambs, plagues and famines became regular possibilities, and Adam's backyard no longer looks like a perfectly manicured, weed-free fairway on the 18th hole at Augusta.

As we've seen already, there has always been disagreement among Christians as to whether or not a devastating hurricane was a direct act of God's judgment on individual sins or whether hurricanes are just part of a fallen world that God providentially upholds and sustains, but if there was one thing most Catholics, Lutherans, and Calvinists agreed on it was that one way or another, even natural evils are a result of Adam and Eve's sin. But throughout the Scientific Revolution and the Enlightenment, this human-centric view of the cosmos faced increased scrutiny. Galileo and Copernicus had rightly questioned a long-held notion that our planet was the center of the universe and proved beyond a shadow of a doubt that the earth revolved around the sun. Our world wasn't the center of it all.

Isaac Newton had proposed that the universe was running on a system of laws like a finely tuned machine. If you sat under an apple tree and a falling apple caused you to get a little knot on your noggin, it wasn't God throwing an apple at you. It was just gravity. So much of the universe, including the very movements of heavenly bodies, were functioning on their own. Planets and galaxies beyond our primitive imaginations were doing just fine without us. For some, like Gottfried Leibniz, the increased scale and magnitude of creation only added to the wonder and beauty of God's creation. For others, it challenged long-held notions that God had made us the central characters in the cosmos. The idea that human shortcomings might be at the center of all of the world's ailments seemed less tenable, and the challenges to it only became more difficult in the 18th and 19th centuries.

Christians had long held to the theological affirmation of the God-given value of both reason and revelation as paths to understanding God and His world. During the Enlightenment, we saw a debate among Christian thinkers about the value of reason in knowing God. For natural theologians like Leibniz, reason was the superior path to understanding God and his world. For others like Kant and Schleiermacher, reason was entirely insufficient to understand God. In the following centuries, Christians convinced that natural theology and reason had immense value in disclosing the truth about God sought to find ways of affirming what they believed the Bible taught about God and his world. They used disciplines like science to attempt to harmonize general revelation and special revelation.

Christian geologists, a relatively new scientific discipline at the time, set out to scour the earth for geological evidence of a global flood hoping to demonstrate the reasonableness of the story of Noah. Could they find evidence of a worldwide catastrophe of this scale? As they studied the earth's horizontal layers of rock and sediment known as *strata*, it became clear that there was a global catastrophe. The only problem was that there wasn't just one global catastrophe but evidence of multiple catastrophes. Not only that, but the geological evidence also seemed to point to geological formations that had been the result of very long, slow processes- processes much older than some of the traditional dating for the origins of Adam and Eve.

One old practice for hypothesizing the age of the earth had been to look at the biblical genealogies listed in the Bible and come up with a rough calculation of how long ago Adam would have lived. According to these calculations, the earth couldn't be older than 6,000-8,000 years, but the findings of these 18-19th century Christian geologists were pointing to an earth that was substantially older.[107] Obviously, this created concerns about the scientific legitimacy of the Bible, but it also created deep psychological, theological, and ethical challenges about the place of humans in creation. If humans only occupied this tiny sliver of time near the end of the geological timeline, and if there clearly was death in the plant and animal world before there could have been an Adam and Eve, can we really say that Adam and Eve's sin brought about natural evil?

While humans in different civilizations before the 19th century uncovered strange fossilized bones of unknown creatures, it wasn't until the 19th century that dinosaur fossils were properly discovered and categorized. The discovery of these dinosaurs made for all sorts of unique challenges for Christians hoping to harmonize science with their interpretation of the Bible. Did Noah simply not like T-Rexes and keep them off the ark? No, that wasn't it. The geological evidence was clear but unsettling- dinosaurs and humans never walked the earth at the same time. How can this be? Wasn't the world a perfectly peaceful, utopian paradise until Adam and Eve's sin? I mean, I've seen *Jurassic Park*, and T-Rexes seem to like killing things and eating them. I thought "*sin entered the world through one man, and death through sin."* (Romans 5:12) Both the legitimacy of the Bible as a reasonable authority and the human-centered story seemed under attack.

In the face of this apparent divide between science and faith, some apologists who held to an Augustinian-styled, human-centered theodicy tried to defend what they thought was the truth of the Bible against the scientific consensus of modern geology. George Bugg was one of those popular apologists, and in 1826 he wrote a book called *Scriptural Geology* that tried to defend the idea that human sin was the cause of all the earth's suffering and death. In that book, he argued that earth was recently created in six literal days, carnivores were originally vegetarian herbivores until Adam's sin, and that, while the Bible is not a science book, science that disagrees with a literal interpretation of the Bible is erroneous.[108] Bugg's work became the blueprint for what we now know today as *young earth creationism.*

Among geologists, Bugg's position was a minority viewpoint. Others attempted to work out other theories about how an old earth teeming with life for eons could be reconciled with the book of Genesis, while others took on the approach of Kant and Schleiermacher and simply abandoned any necessary correspondence between general revelation and special revelation. This book does not set out to settle science and faith issues. I have addressed some of these issues elsewhere.[109] What's most important to our journey at the present moment is understanding the implications of the 19th-century debate. If suffering and evil in the natural world aren't a part of the penalty for human sin, then what is it? Could we really call God's creation good if, long before human sin, there were already millions upon millions of years of death and decay?

Defending the goodness of God and his creation became even more difficult after the publication of Charles Darwin's *Origin of Species* in 1859. In 1831, the British Empire sent out a ten-gun naval battleship on a five-year mission, the *HMS*

Beagle, to explore South America, New Zealand, and Australia. Aboard the HMS Beagle was a young scientist named Charles Darwin. Darwin originally went to school to be a minister, but his personal experiences of suffering and the suffering he observed in the natural world on his voyage to the Galapagos Islands created an insurmountable problem for the Christian conceptions of God he once had as a boy.[110]

Darwin's scientific investigations into the natural world produced a convincing scientific theory that all of the variation of plant and animal life we see throughout the world was the result of genetic adaptations that increased the likelihood of survival for those plants and animals in a very competitive and often violent world. Traits that increase the likelihood of survival get passed on, while traits that decrease the likelihood of survival or are just plain inefficient eventually get weeded out. One of the most disturbing examples of what Darwin thought was the inherently violent nature of evolution could be found in the ichneumon wasp. This wasp lays its eggs inside another animal's body, like the fictional xenomorphs in the *Alien* movie franchise. As the eggs hatch inside of, say, a caterpillar, they slowly eat their way through the caterpillar, saving the most vital of organs for last so that the caterpillar does not die too soon and begin to decay before the cute baby ichneumons can eat their fill. Survival of the fittest can be a grizzly affair.

In 1860, Darwin wrote to his friend Asa Gray that his study of the natural world had led him to a crisis of faith.[111] What kind of God makes a world with ichneumon wasps? Darwin's work deepened the theodicy problem. If God created *ex nihilo* and this method of evolution, where only the strong survive, was God's way of producing all the diversity of life on this planet, how can this God be good? And if humans aren't some special act of creation, but products of the same evolutionary processes, with apes as evolutionary predecessors, then how do we make any sense of the Bible at all?

Some in Darwin's day accepted his scientific research but

questioned his interpretative language. One such person was a geologist, paleontologist, and priest named William Buckland. Buckland thought the young earth apologetics of George Bugg were terribly mistaken. It's foolish to deny the overwhelming scientific evidence of biology and geology just because it doesn't fit your interpretation of the Bible. Theologians should wrestle with geology and Darwin's findings, not deny them. While many Christians in the 19th century saw the new science as a threat to faith, Buckland thought it was "marvelous" that there were so many new things for humanity to discover about God's creation. Where some might have looked at the catastrophe that killed off the dinosaurs as senseless violence or the evolutionary history filled with predation and death as a challenge to belief in the God of the Bible, Buckland saw God's hand of providence continually adapting the world for increased human benefit.[112]

He believed that all suffering serves the universal good. Death was an inevitable experience for all organic beings and part of God's proper design of the cosmos. Physical death and decomposition weren't punishments traceable to the fall of Adam; they were just part of the functional ordering of creation. Humanity's sin does create suffering, but it primarily creates instances of suffering in *how* we relate to other humans directly. A man that steals from his neighbor creates suffering for his neighbor and eventually himself, but that sin isn't responsible for the existence of a devastating hurricane. A hurricane exists not because humanity fell and sinned but because they are just part of God's mysterious, grand ordering of the universe.[113]

Awareness of the violence and suffering of the natural world didn't originate with Darwin's work. Naturalists long before Darwin had observed a similar phenomenon. A generation before Darwin, the natural theologian and minister William Paley observed similar features in nature but considered it a "myriad of happy beings" living in balance.[114] While much of Darwin's science seemed airtight, his descriptive language was far from neutral or purely objective. Darwinian theory in subsequent generations became reducible by many to "survival of the fittest." This seemed to have an inherent bias towards negativity- a negativity that other Christians like Paley and Buckland just didn't see as they looked out on the natural world.

Nevertheless, Christians have continued to wrestle with the scientific discoveries and language of the 19th century. One path taken by some Christians was the George Bugg method- let's create an alternative science that fits a more traditional Augustinian framework and our way of interpreting the Bible. Others sought to make sense of God and the world through both the science of the day and the timeless theological truths of Scripture. Still, like Darwin near the end of his life, others felt that science revealed a depth to the problem of evil that was simply too much for their faith to bear.

To those who may find themselves in that last category, allow me to offer you a word of encouragement at this point in our tour:

Don't give up.

I have seen too many abandon their Christian faith for what they believe is a "more reasonable" view of the world in what we could call *modern scientism,* only to find that the problem of evil and suffering doesn't just go away but just gets worse. Many who continue to follow the trajectory of their questions within that framework find only nihilism at the end of the road. It was a concern that the noted German atheist Freidrich Nietzsche voiced when he wrote in 1882 his infamous "Parable of the Madman" in a book entitled *The Gay Science.*

> "Have you not heard of that madman who lit a lantern in the bright morning hours, ran to the marketplace, and cried incessantly: "I seek God! I seek God!" -- As many of those who did not believe in God were standing around just then, he provoked much laughter. Has he got lost? asked one. Did he

lose his way like a child? asked another. Or is he hiding? Is he afraid of us? Has he gone on a voyage? emigrated? -- Thus they yelled and laughed.

The madman jumped into their midst and pierced them with his eyes. "Whither is God?" he cried; "I will tell you. We have killed him -- you and I. All of us are his murderers. But how did we do this? How could we drink up the sea? Who gave us the sponge to wipe away the entire horizon? What were we doing when we unchained this earth from its sun? Whither is it moving now? Whither are we moving? Away from all suns? Are we not plunging continually? Backward, sideward, forward, in all directions? Is there still any up or down? Are we not straying, as through an infinite nothing? Do we not feel the breath of empty space? Has it not become colder? Is not night continually closing in on us? Do we not need to light lanterns in the morning? Do we hear nothing as yet of the noise of the gravediggers who are burying God? Do we smell nothing as yet of the divine decomposition? Gods, too, decompose. God is dead. God remains dead. And we have killed him.

How shall we comfort ourselves, the murderers of all murderers? What was holiest and mightiest of all that the world has yet owned has bled to death under our knives: who will wipe this blood off us? What water is there for us to clean ourselves? What festivals of atonement, what sacred games shall we have to invent? Is not the greatness of this deed too great for us?

Must we ourselves not become gods simply to appear worthy of it? There has never been a greater deed; and whoever is born after us -- for the sake of this deed he will belong to a higher history than all history hitherto.

Here the madman fell silent and looked again at his listeners; and they, too, were silent and stared at him in astonishment. At last he threw his lantern on the ground, and it broke into pieces and went out. "I have come too early," he said then; "my time is not yet. This tremendous event is still on its way, still wandering; it has not yet reached the ears of men. Lightning and thunder require time; the light of the stars requires time; deeds, though done, still require time to be seen and heard. This deed is still more distant from them than most distant stars -- and yet they have done it themselves.

It has been related further that on the same day the madman forced his way into several churches and there struck up his requiem aeternam deo. Led out and called to account, he is said always to have replied nothing but: "What after all are these churches now if they are not the tombs and sepulchers of God?"[115]

Nietzsche believed that by the end of the 19th century, the Western world had killed God. Maybe the problem of evil was more than what the Christian story could bear? The news of God's death had not quite hit the mainstream. Though Nietzsche was an atheist, he was deeply concerned about what would happen when that day finally arrived. What would become of the world if *survival of the fittest* moved from being descriptive to *prescriptive*? Decades after Nietzsche, German civilization would take *survival of the fittest* from a scientific *is* to a political and ethical *ought*. Maybe killing God doesn't solve the problem of evil at all.

14. KARL BARTH: CHAOS, CHRIST, & THE SHADOWSIDE OF GOD'S WILL

As the madman's announcement of the death of God spread throughout the West, the world found itself plunged into two great conflicts, the likes of which transcended all of humanity's prior conflicts. This was the beginning of the age of nihilism. Maybe the problem of evil had won. Maybe we are hopelessly lost.

In the midst of those two great wars, a Swiss Reformed theologian named Karl Barth argued that God was paradoxically most found when he appeared to be most hidden. Barth was a preacher and theology professor from Basel, Switzerland. Initially, Barth studied theology within the growing movement of Protestant Liberalism but became disenfranchised by the movement when his theological mentor, Adoph Von Harnack, signed off on the "Manifesto of the Ninety Three German Intellectuals to the Civilized World." This document expressed support of the German military actions early in World War I- actions commonly referred to as the "Rape of Belgium." If this was the fruit of liberal theology, Barth wanted nothing to do with it.[116]

Before Hitler seized power in Germany in 1933, Barth was already a vocal opponent of the Nazi movement. In 1934, Barth was a key leader in writing the Barmen Declaration, which was a scathing theological rebuke of Nazi ideology, Christian nationalism, and the unholy matrimony of German churches and Nazism. Barth didn't do this on some fake burner Twitter account where he could just get some stuff off his chest and then evade all ramifications. He personally mailed a copy of the Barmen Declaration to Adolf Hitler.[117] Barth was eventually kicked out of Germany after refusing to pledge allegiance to Hitler. He settled back home in Switzerland and continued teaching systematic theology at the University of Basel until his retirement in 1962.

Barth was no stranger to the challenges that natural evil presented to the discipline of natural theology, and he was personally acquainted with the horrors of human moral evil that he saw all around him during the two world wars. As one of the most influential theologians of the 20th century, how did Barth address the problem of evil and suffering? First, Barth rejected the Enlightenment's emphasis on reason and natural theology as the primary path to knowing God. Barth saw the growing emphasis on natural theology in the 19th and 20th-century Protestant liberalism as completely misguided. These theologians looking for God in immanence forget that God is wholly transcendent and wholly other than the creation. Those looking for knowledge of God in the natural world are misguided because knowledge of the transcendent God comes only in revelation.[118] In that way, we can see Barth in a line of prior Christian thinkers such as Luther and the Pietist-influenced Kant and Schleiermacher (albeit with some very sharp differences).

Barth most directly addresses the problem of evil in Volume 3 of his *Church Dogmatics* - a massive thirteen-volume systematic theology written over the course of 30 years. The ambition, scope, and influence of Church Dogmatics as a systematic theology may only be rivaled by Thomas Aquinas's *Summa Theologica* and John Calvin's *Institutes of the Christian Religion*. This particular volume was written between 1948 and

1950, not long after the conclusion of World War II. With the radical evils of World War II in mind, Barth insists that there must be some sort of "alien factor" at work in creation. He calls this sinister force *das Nichtige*, loosely translated into English as "that which is not."[119]

Barth believes the formlessness and voidness described in Genesis 1:2 to be the primordial chaos of all the possibilities that God chose not to make an actuality. This Nothingness is that which attempts to cause separation in the relationship between humanity and God. Barth believes there's a twofold character to God's created order. Light and dark, growth and decay, a yes for one and a no for another, are all just part of God's good ordering of reality. The darkness and decay, along with the temporary pain and suffering accompanying them, are simply the *"shadowside"* of God's will. Challenging prior Augustinian-influenced interpretations of the Fall, Barth argues that physical decay and death are not evil but are simply part of the shadowside process of God's will in creation. The Fall, however, was not part of the functional, shadowside order of creation but was humanity's choice of *das Nichtige* instead of God's will. The shadowside of creation still has a right-ordering to its purpose. *Das Nichtige* is unordered chaos.[120]

Dying of old age isn't evil; it's the shadowside of God's good creation. Dying in the gas chambers at Auschwitz is *das Nichtige*; it's the potentiality that God rejects for creation but a chaos that moral agents can still choose. For Barth, this is what makes sin so insidious. The sinner is effectively saying that they know *what should be* better than the Creator by choosing to bring about what God has rejected. Now, if this is your first exposure to Karl Barth, you might wonder, "Um, this *das Nichtige* business sounds like evil might be an ontological rival to God. Is this guy a Gnostic?" To stay in keeping with his Reformed tradition, Barth attempts to avoid Gnostic hyper-dualism by vehemently denying that this Nothingness and chaos is a genuine rival to the sovereignty of God. Admittedly, his attempts to do this while still trying not to make evil a function of God's sovereignty, like some perceived in the work of Calvin, are confusing.

In some places, Barth argues that *das Nichtige* is "utterly distinct from Creator and creation...the antithesis which is not merely within creation and therefore dialectical but which is primarily and supremely the antithesis to God himself," while in other places he writes that *das Nichtige* is "is not a second God, nor self-created."[121] As we've seen, this is not a new tension in Christian theology.

How do we seriously assign blame for evil and unjust suffering on forces that are not God while not making them a rival to God? At times, Barth's language pushes just beyond the moderate cosmic dualism of the early Church Fathers like Justin Martyr and Ireneaus. But Barth differs from those early Christian voices by arguing that the demonic is not the result of some angelic fall, but that demons simply emerge from the chaotic *das Nichtige*. We need not give much energy speculating on their origins because what's most important to Barth is that we simply affirm that these principalities and powers exist and commit to having no partnership with them whatsoever.[122]

So what does Barth make of the work of Christ, and how does it relate to *das Nichtige*, the shadowside of creation, and the suffering we see both in the natural world and from human moral agents? In his commentary on Romans, Barth makes clear that trying to deduce God's character and nature via reason or nature is essentially worthless. Humanity cannot know God from the bottom-up, but only from the top-down through the revelation of Jesus Christ. Jesus Christ, whom the Scriptures bear witness to, is the only Word of God. Only through the light of Christ can we begin to know God in His creation properly.

Those perplexed by the previously unimaginable levels of violence and suffering described by modern geology and Darwinian evolution have a way to counter the conundrum. According to Barth, the sciences have nothing to say about God. Only Christ tells us what's true about God. Once a person is in Christ, they can begin to correctly interpret the world because they have the hermeneutic key. Any other effort outside of Christ to understand God is useless religion and part of a bottom-up attempt by the self-righteous to justify themselves. Proper theology is the top-down, self-disclosure of a gracious God to humanity in Jesus Christ.

Drawing upon those theological voices before him that attempted to place revelation above reason, Barth argued that without Christ, we cannot properly interpret the shadowside of creation. Evidence for God's existence or Jesus 'lordship is ambiguous at best. In fact, if we were to try and make a pros and cons list for why we should have faith in God, we wouldn't even be able to know what a pro or con, a good or bad, is outside of the light of Christ. For Barth, it is only by the light of Christ that we can adequately distinguish between what is good, what is the shadowside of God's goodness, and what is genuinely *das Nichtige*.

Christ saves humanity from our trajectory toward nothingness. Because Jesus was completely obedient to the Father's will, He never participated in *das Nichtige*, therefore our participation in Christ through faith intercepts the trajectory we once had towards the chaos and nothingness of *das Nichtige* and reroutes us into properly ordered union with God. But once again, like Luther, Barth believes that we only come to know this as true by the grace of God through faith. There is a paradoxical hiddenness to God's self-disclosure. A crucified Christ doesn't make much sense if you're looking for a reasonable picture of an omnipotent God, but this is why, like Luther, Barth believes we need to shift away from metaphysical speculations about evil and focus more on the proper response to evil that a life in Christ calls us to.

Barth once wrote, "The true God is the hidden God."[123] It is in the suffering and crucified messiah where we find God's perfect source of self-disclosure. In the suffering of the Cross and the vindication of the resurrection, we can find out how to existentially address our own experiences of suffering. That God in Christ tasted of human suffering should come as great consolation, according to Barth.

In the spring of 1941, Karl Barth's twenty-year-old son Mattias died after a rock climbing accident. They say that a parent should never have to bury their child. Not only did Barth do this, but he chose to preach the sermon at his son's funeral. The Scripture text he preached from was evidently a favorite passage of his son. 1 Corinthians 13:12, in the German translation Barth read from, says, "For now we see through a glass, in an enigmatic word, but then face to face." Trying to summarize a sermon from such a devastating moment in someone's life does not feel appropriate. Instead, I have selected some key sections that may give the best possible window into Barth's theodicy, not merely described in a systematic theology book, but in the living practice of one of the hardest moments of his life.

> "Because God's grace has come to help us in our misery through our Lord and Savior Jesus Christ, thus it is so: wherever and however we live our life with all its hopes, weaknesses, and secrets, both are true, both—deeply and indissolubly united with each other: the Now! but also the Then! They are not separate from each other but entirely together: The Now where we see very well and understand everything, yet we do not know at all what everything is like in reality. And the Then, where we will see everything clearly and where all will be glorious. The Now: a mirror in which everything is turned upside down; an enigmatic word, which certainly gives us an answer but at the same time remains the most difficult question. And the Then: where we will not only be known by God, but we ourselves will know him no less fully than he knows us...

It is by the grace of our Lord Jesus Christ that the Now and the Then are together in such a way that no power in heaven or on earth can separate them again. For it is he alone who in his bitter death on the cross and in his glorious resurrection has bound the Now and the Then together so that even now there is no mirror or enigmatic word that does not have standing behind it the clarity of that seeing face to face. And everything single beaming ray of the future glory of God will be nothing but a particular turning and adjusting of the reflection before which we now stand, a particular resolving of the riddle we are now trying to figure out.

...In our thoughts about our Matthias we do not want to put ourselves in any other place than precisely at this border. He has now crossed over it, and we are still here. But we are not far from each other if we put ourselves at this border. But we are not far from each other if we put ourselves at this border. In Jesus Christ there is no distance between Now and Then, between here and there, however profoundly they are separated. Our Matthias—just as he really was—is in Jesus Christ, yet very differently than the way he used to live with us and we with him. He is the same, yet he has become completely different. Because Jesus Christ has taught us about both, about life and death, death and life, we may now therefore remember our

Matthias and thus speak about him."[124]

As we can see in Barth's funeral sermon, living between the Now and the Then of the Kingdom of God, our attempts to understand the evil and suffering of this world will ultimately be incomplete. What Christ offers us instead is a living hope in the final setting right of all things. To be in Christ means to be people positioned smack-dab on the boundary of the Now and the Yet to Come. After that final culmination, the enigmatic reflection of this cloudy mirror we now look upon will be properly adjusted to present a picture of pristine clarity.

As with all of our previous theodicies, Barth's theodicy is not without its critics. One critique of Barth's theodicy is how difficult it would be for someone to sort through the differences between the shadowside of God's will and *das Nichtige*. Is a pandemic that causes lock-downs that, in turn, temporarily decrease the output of harmful pollutants that damage the earth's environment, part of the shadowside of God's will keeping the equilibrium of the planet in functional balance, or is it an insidious natural evil of *das Nichtige* responsible for the unnecessary deaths of millions of image bearers? Secondly, does Barth's low view of general revelation ultimately place too strong of an emphasis on the fallenness of creation and its lack of intelligibility, and does it undercut God's decree of the inherent goodness of the world He made?

Some may find Barth's low view of natural theology helpful in light of Darwinian evolution. After all, there's no need to defend or deny evolutionary theory if nature doesn't truly reveal God. Others see it as an unnecessary rift in the modes by which we can learn the truth about God and his world. Are we really forced to believe that Christ is unreasonable? What are we supposed to make of the scientific advances of the 20th century that contributed to a 60% increase in life expectancy? Didn't millions of scientists without a professing-faith in Jesus Christ use their faculties of reason to contribute to the flourishing of humanity in ways that Christians and non-Christians would agree are good?

Supporters of Barth's theodicy would likely respond by saying that we only know that these advancements that improve the quality of life are good if the light of Christ serves as our ethical north star. After all, the Nazis thought they were using science for good when running eugenics experiments. How are we to say that they were wrong, especially when they were attempting to make a human race more fit for survival?

Perhaps Barth's lasting contribution to theodicy was his emphasis on a God who suffers too, influencing a young fiery American preacher named Martin Luther King Jr. Whether it was with those in the gas chambers of the Holocaust or those mourning at a funeral the death of a young man such as Barth's own son, these moments of pain and suffering may be the most profound moments of tangible grace, sitting in the border between here and there, between Now and the Yet to Come. Because God's truest self-disclosure is found in a crucified Messiah, it may be in the place of suffering where the revelation of God in Christ is most deeply experienced.

15. PROCESS THEISM & OPEN THEISM: IS POSSIBILITY POSSIBLE?

Perhaps at this point in our journey you feel as if you found a satisfactory theodicy from one or more of the Christian voices of the past. Others of you may still be unsettled or unsatisfied with the aforementioned options. Either way, you can hopefully see that even by the 20th century there was no single theodicy in the Christian tradition that satisfied all parties. Maybe it was time to consider far more creative approaches.

In two unique theological movements known as *Process Theism* and *Open Theism*, philosophers and theologians attempted to consider possible solutions to the problem of evil that would move beyond the normal bounds of classical theism, natural theology, and even Molinism. Were these novel theologies an improvement? Did they move too far away from historical conceptions of God and His created order to even be considered part of the Christian tradition? Were they even that novel to begin with, or were they simply updated packaging to much older ideas? Let's explore these innovative attempts together in this chapter.

∗∗∗

As the "suffering God" theodicies first popularized by Karl Barth grew in acceptance, a British mathematician and philosopher named Alfred North Whitehead was working through his own metaphysical system that could make sense of a suffering God and also square with new mathematical and scientific discoveries such as quantum mechanics. Whitehead believed that early in the development of Christian thought, as Christianity expanded and interacted with Greek philosophy, that the ancient thinkers misunderstood the essential nature of reality. To Whitehead, reality itself is always in a state of flux. There is a perpetual becoming that is essential to reality itself. Things come to be and then they pass away. Christian theology and most modern philosophy had wrongly focused on *being* instead of *becoming*, and Whitehead sought to remedy that.[125]

Immutability, impassibility, omnipotence, and omniscience were philosophical deductions of Greek philosophy imposed on the Christian God of the Bible. Whitehead believed that this kind of "Unmoved-Mover" couldn't be squared with the nature of the ever-changing reality of quantum mechanics or with the biblical portrayal of God as emotionally moved, immanent, and even, at times, limited in his knowledge of future outcomes. Disciples of Whitehead believed that his new metaphysics known as *process philosophy, process thought,* or *Process Theism* would be the "solution [that] dissolves the problem of evil."[126]

To understand how some process theists believe that this creative philosophy eliminates the problem of evil, we'll need to spend some time unpacking these complex metaphysical proposals. As is the case in previous chapters where we've done some philosophical groundwork before properly diving into the implications on our questions surrounding evil and suffering, we really can't shortcut the philosophical process in this chapter (yes, pun intended) if we're really going to grasp the possible strengths and weaknesses of Process Theism on the subject of God, evil, and suffering.

Whitehead believed that everything in existence is made up of tiny droplets of experience called *entities*. Every single entity is in a state of becoming with its own aims and goals. Whitehead believed that God was an entity also in a state of becoming, but the biggest difference between God and other entities is that God is the only everlasting entity and that God provides the best possible outcome for each entity.[127] That God is in process too, along with creation, is a feature of process thought that radically differs from classical Christian theism.

Whitehead believed that God had a "dipolar" nature that consisted of an unchanging, *primordial nature* and an ever-changing *consequent nature*.[128] The first nature is, in one sense, unchanging and made up of all the possibilities that reality could become. God is the source of all entities. This side of God's nature is similar to classical conceptions of God in the classic tradition. For example, this side of God's nature can't truly make decisions. He is beyond decision-making and unchangeable. In fact, Whitehead believed it was not accurate to say that God decided to make creation. Creation necessarily exists along with God because otherwise, God would not eternally be Creator.

This is another substantial point of difference between Process Theism and classical Christian theism. Process theists deny that creation came to be out of nothing, but rather there is a primordial creative energy that has to be given a direction. The primordial nature of God provides creativity its aims, but He cannot decide how creation unfolds. While Process Theism is a diverse school of thought, most process theists would agree with Whitehead's belief that God cannot act coercively to direct or control creation. Creation goes where it wills, and God's only influence on its direction is through the attractiveness of His beauty and goodness.

That second part of God's nature, the consequent nature,

is considered to be the eternal now of every moment, experiencing everything in reality as it happens in every changing moment. This part of God's nature is that part that allows Whitehead and other process theists to believe that God actually suffers with his creation as it suffers. Christian process theists (as there are many other kinds of process theists) often point to this complex dipolar natures in God as the best way they can make sense of the God revealed in Scripture who apparently suffers, experiences emotion, gives conditional predictions on the choices of human moral agents, and is moved by our prayers and worship.[129]

Other popular process theologians include Charles Hartshorne, David Ray Griffin, John Cobb, Joseph Bracken, and Thomas Jay Oord, to name a few. Though these men have their fair share of subtle disagreement, they all agree with Whitehead that the various schools of classical Christian thought, whether it's from Augustine, Aquinas, Luther, or Calvin, inevitably made God the source of evil by claiming that God was unchangeable and omnipotent. While God provides the ultimate ethical vision, "creativity" is the true ontological ultimate. The Catholic process theologian Joseph Bracken argues in *Christianity and Process Thought: Spirituality for a Changing World* that we should consider creativity as a force "even more ultimate than God."[130] As detestable as this may initially sound to many of you, consider their counterargument.

In his sovereignty and omnipotence, could God act right now to end all evil and every instance of suffering (a question popularized by David Ray Griffin)? If you say yes, are you confessing that God simply does not want to end evil and suffering? Or, to put it another way, are you suggesting that God is willing that evil and suffering exist? Yikes. That's a tricky question. If you say no, and believe that God could not just decide to end all evil and suffering at this very moment, then it seems that you believe that God answers to some other power. It's like we're suddenly back to ol 'Epicurus 'original quandary about an all-powerful and all-good God.

Process theists argue that their philosophy makes better sense of the unique theodicy problems brought about by dinosaurs and Darwin in the 19th century. If God cannot unilaterally act in the world to bring about His desired creation, then we should expect a long, violent process of creation. Throw in the fact that God does not create *ex nihilo* but instead has to work with pre-existent chaos and the primordial creative energy fundamental to existence, and we should expect an imperfect creation that goes through a long, arduous process of change and adaptation. Natural evils are just part of the inherent unpredictability of creativity at work in nature.

How does process theism attempt to address the causes of human moral evils? Because humans have genuine freedom of will and God cannot intervene to coerce them to do what He wants, humans are free to use the force of creativity in a way that goes against God's hopes for creation. Process theists believe that their view makes better sense of human moral evils and vindicates God from any culpability by saying that God is simply powerless to intervene in instances of murder, theft, rape, or abuse.

Some critics of process thought argue that Process Theism isn't really that new at all and that it may just be an updated variation of an ancient rival to orthodox Christianity. Remember that ancient Gnosticism taught that beyond the cosmos, at the source of our material or phenomenal reality, there were two competing forces responsible for creation. The apparent deficiencies of the world, including all of the evil and suffering, could be blamed on an imperfect demiurge. Remember that this was a compelling theodicy because it allowed for the existence of an all-good supreme God as the ethical source of truth, goodness, and beauty. The Gnostics supposedly solved the problem of evil by saying that the God in charge of our messed-up creation wasn't really in charge. To put it another way, if the explanation for why evil exists is a choice between either "God's not all-powerful" or "God's not all good," the Gnostics were rolling with a lack of power. Is Process Theism really doing anything different than this?

Critics of Process Theism have some strong questions about whether or not their perspective is just as radically dualistic as the Gnostics. Is "Creativity" ontologically ultimate with the personal God of the Bible just a limited demiurge? Is a dipolar God really just a God and a demiurge? If Creativity is necessary and God is contingent on creativity, then by definition, isn't Creativity actually God? If God is subject to the same processes of creativity as humanity and is powerless to intervene in stopping evil, then how is this God good in any meaningful way, and how can we ever even trust in anything like a final setting right of creation?

Still, others who support process metaphysics have argued that as different as it is from the classical views, it is a philosophy that is much more compatible with the Bible than the views held by Augustine, Aquinas, or even Molina. If God is immutable, as in the classical view, how can the God of the Bible express so much pain or anger as we see with the Old Testament prophets? Why is it that God even calls humans to cooperate in his purposes for the world? Why is there conditional prophecy throughout the Bible if possibility isn't genuinely possible? How does a God that transcends time and is beyond change not logically lead one to conclude that God is the impersonal "clock-maker" God of Deism? These are all legitimate counter-questions.

Process theists see the immanence and changeability of God as offering comfort to those who are suffering. After all, this kind of God suffers just like you and me. But there's an even deeper question about whether or not a changeable God should really be seen as a comfort to those who are suffering or facing evil. If the world is making God just as much as God is making the world, and if there is no end but rather an eternal process of becoming, then aren't we left without the ability to define what good or evil is?

If God can morally evolve, and some process theists see

the difference between a God who sponsors wars in the Old Testament and a God who tells people to love their enemies in the New Testament as evidence of God morally evolving, then ethical right and wrong cannot be found in God's unchanging character and must be located elsewhere. But where? Could it be possible that one day we learn along with God that the Holocaust wasn't actually bad? It seems impossible to know if God is becoming and not being, whether or not something like the Holocaust isn't simply the new good that has emerged out of the process of becoming. And who would get to speak on behalf of God and give us these new ethics?

No matter what you think about Process Theism, whether you think the old classical metaphysics are untouchable, needs to be challenged, or you'd be fine never reading the word *metaphysics* again, it is probably safe to say that some process theists have oversold their ability to solve the problem of evil. There are clearly some legitimate challenges to its coherence. One undeniable effect of the process critique of God as unlimited power was that it encouraged a new crop of Christian philosophers and theologians to explore other creative alternatives to both the classical view and the new process view. One of these new schools of Christian thought that developed in the late 20th century became known as Open Theism.

In an effort to devise a metaphysical system that could make sense of a God who suffers with his suffering creation, process theists rejected many of the classical conceptions of God as immutable, impassible, omniscient, and omnipotent. Most Catholic and Protestant theologians alike felt that the process view had too many fatal flaws. But some Protestant Evangelical theologians in the late 20th century believed that several of the critiques by process thinkers of the classical view had some merit. Maybe ideas like impossibility, omniscience, and timelessness were more a product of Greek philosophy than biblical revelation?

In these predominantly evangelical circles, debates about God's providence and foreknowledge, which were commonly labeled, quite sloppily, as merely "Calvinism vs. Arminianism debates" frustrated some theologians. It seemed that no matter what side of the debate you picked, possibility didn't seem genuinely possible. And if possibility isn't genuinely possible, then there can be no free will.

Here's an illustration I used to demonstrate with my students in the classroom that would always get them thinking (if it didn't drive them insane first):

Imagine I'm standing in front of you and offer you the choice between a stapler in one hand and a pen in the other hand. There is no follow-up task I assign to you that will require one of these two tools. It is an entirely arbitrary decision. Now, before you make your selection, I ask, "Does God know which one you will choose?" Both John Calvin and Jacob Arminius would answer with a resounding "yes!" For Calvin, God knew because He predestined it by eternal divine decree. For Arminius, God knew because God perfectly foreknew all things. If you answered "yes," then the question becomes, "Well, when did he know which object you will choose?"

The most common answer I got from my Christian students was something along the lines of "before the beginning of time." So before I even grabbed this pen and stapler, God knew I would do so? Before any student enrolled in this class, God knew they would do so? Before the students or I existed, God knew that we would exist? Before my parents got married and conceived me, God knew that they would? On and on, we could go.

I then ask you to make a choice- pen or stapler? Let's say you reach out and select the stapler. If God eternally and perfectly foreknew that you would choose the stapler, could you have chosen the pen? Could you have chosen a different school?

Could my parents have chosen a different spouse?

One of the most common responses I would get from students was, "Well, I could have changed my mind at the last second and chosen the pen. God knowing it doesn't mean that I had to do it." To which my provocative response was, "Well, when did God know that you would change your mind? A second before? An hour? Or before the foundations of the world?" Hopefully, you can see the problem. If God has perfect foreknowledge of everything, then don't you have to do what God perfectly knew you would do? The pen isn't actually an option for you. It just appears to be. If that is true, then there really is no meaningful difference between foreknowledge and predestination.

How can possibility truly be possible? It seemed to this new group of theologians troubled by both the classical view and Process Theism, that the entire biblical narrative would collapse if there weren't a way to logically affirm the real existence of possibility and genuine free will. The picture of God from Augustine to Calvin seemed like a God who acted as an arsonist firefighter, decreeing evil only to elicit some sense of glory when He saved us from the fire He started.

In 1980, a Seventh Day Adventist theologian named Richard Rice wrote what many consider to be the first book on Open Theism entitled *The Openness of God: The Relationship Between Divine Foreknowledge and Human Free Will*.[131] The core problem that Rice attempted to address was the problem of divine foreknowledge and free will. While Rice's book may have been the first to contain the phrase "open theism," it wasn't until 1994 and a book co-authored by Rice along with Clark Pinnock, John Sanders, William Hasker, and David Bassinger entitled *The Openness of God: A Biblical Challenge to the Traditional Understanding of God* came along that Open Theism would take the world of academic theology, and eventually the evangelical church world, by controversial storm.

These open theists argued that both classical theism

and process theism had forced the biblical revelation into a particular philosophical system instead of adapting a philosophical system to work within the confines of the biblical revelation.[132] What would happen if we tried to derive a suitable philosophical structure from the biblical data first? What would be the essential ingredients?

Though there are a variety of open theists, just as there are classical theists and process theists, we could still point to some essential affirmations that evangelical open theists, who tried to hold to the primacy of the Scriptures, espoused. First, human moral responsibility is critical to the Biblical narrative. If we can't figure out a way for humans to be responsible for their actions in the world, then concepts such as the Fall, sin, and even repentance and redemption make no sense. Second, God is personal and desires genuine, loving relational communion with humanity. Third (and this point is probably most strongly made by another godfather of Open Theism, Greg Boyd), the ministry of Jesus who we see healing the sick, raising the dead, casting out demons, and even calling Satan the "prince of this world" must really be redemptive and rescuing acts- not God acting as the arsonist who starts the fire and then, in Christ, puts it out as the firefighter expecting us to see it as a genuine rescue. [133]

With these core convictions, evangelical open theists set out to challenge what they perceived as the philosophical constraints of classical Christian metaphysics and the theology that they believed undercut the biblical revelation. First, if human moral responsibility is essential to the integrity of the biblical narrative, then possibility has to be genuinely possible. If you couldn't actually choose the pen over the stapler, then you aren't really responsible for that choice. If everything from the innocuous choice of what shirt you wore today to whether or not you become a serial killer or a nun with your life is settled by divine foreordination, then how are you responsible for any of it? Open theists argue that there must be some sort of misunderstanding of what constitutes God's omniscience. God can't know what you will choose between the pen or the stapler until you choose it.

Some open theists would say that it is within God's power to limit His own knowledge, allowing for the real possibility of undetermined human decisions. Other open theists would say that God limiting His own knowledge is an odd logical contradiction. Did He know all of history at one point and then decide to restrict His knowledge later? That doesn't make much sense. Instead, this branch of open theists, including pastor and theologian Greg Boyd, argues that it would be better to consider their view an *open view of the future* where God simply structures reality in such a way that He intentionally includes possibilities to exist. In this view, God knows all of the actualities that are settled and the contingent possibilities that are open to moral agents to actualize. That which remains open as genuine possibilities do not become actualities to be definitively known until moral agents choose them.[134]

Proponents of the open view point to passages of Scripture that seem to support the existence of conditional possibilities with unknowable outcomes even to God. For example, in Exodus 4 as God is giving Moses commands about how he is supposed to communicate God's plan to free Israel from Egyptian bondage God says, "If they do not believe you or pay attention to the first sign, they may believe the second. But if they do not believe these two signs or listen to you, take some water from the Nile and pour it on the dry ground. The water you take from the river will become blood on the ground." Another common example of conditional prophecy commonly cited by open theists is Jeremiah 18:7-11:

> *If at any time I announce that a nation or kingdom is to be uprooted, torn down and destroyed, and if that nation I warned repents of its evil, then I will relent and not inflict on it the disaster I had planned. And if at another*

time I announce that a nation or kingdom is to be built up and planted, and if it does evil in my sight and does not obey me, then I will reconsider the good I had intended to do for it. Now therefore say to the people of Judah and those living in Jerusalem, 'This is what the Lord says: Look! I am preparing a disaster for you and devising a plan against you. So turn from your evil ways, each one of you, and reform your ways and your actions.

The open theist will ask how God can present conditional prophecies if He definitely knows the outcomes. What would be the point of Him doing so if they couldn't actually change potential outcomes? Wouldn't it be fair to say that God doesn't know how these things will turn out?

Obviously, this presents provocative challenges to traditional understandings of God, but the open theist ardently argues that these notions of God should be challenged by the biblical witness. How can God be immutable and impassible when He clearly presents situations in the Bible where His plans were changed? How can He be beyond being affected by creation when we see the biblical prophets present Him as emotionally moved by people's behavior? To the open theist, Scripture presents a God who is omniscient but only knows what can be known. Possibilities aren't actualities to be known until they become an actuality through free choice.

In Open Theism, it is free will that accounts for both human moral evils and natural evils. Especially in the Open Theism of Clark Pinnock and Greg Boyd, even angelic moral agents have freedom of the will and can use their spiritual potency to influence and affect our material world.[135] Demonic powers can wrongly use their potentiality to bring about diseases and natural disasters. Boyd sees evidence of this throughout the Gospels where Jesus 'healing ministry and even his rebuking of the storm are proof of nefarious powers that rebel against the will of God. Boyd calls this a "warfare worldview" and emphasizes that Christ's work on the Cross and in the Resurrection is primarily about God's victory over malevolent powers of darkness. [136]

Open Theists like to emphasize that what makes God most God is not his supremacy of power but his supremacy of love. God is sovereign, but that doesn't mean every instance of every moment goes the way he would prefer it to go. Open theists can truly say that something as horrific as the Holocaust was never a part of God's plan. Classical theists and process theists alike have their qualms with the open view. First, there are obvious discrepancies in what we should see as essential to the biblical narrative. Can we ever sincerely say that we can build a philosophy purely out of just the Scriptures? Don't we already come to the Bible with biases and inherited philosophies that we can't just shut off on a whim? How would we weigh which biblical texts should be foundational when it appears that there are some passages that seem to point to God changing His mind and responding to contingent possibilities while others, such as Ephesians 1, seem to communicate ideas such as God, "chose us in him before the creation of the world to be holy and blameless in his sight. In love he predestined us for adoption to sonship through Jesus Christ, in accordance with his pleasure and will"? How do you decide which one of those biblical texts is the essential foundational text?

Another question critics of open theism have is about whether or not God can learn. If there are things that God does not yet know, when does God begin to know them? It's not like there's a singular "moment" of decision that happens when we're making a decision. In fact, psychologists at the University of New South Wales using fMRI technology asked study participants to make a choice between two images and were able to detect patterns of brain activity that revealed what their choice would be up to 11 seconds before they made the selection.[137] So when do we actually decide something?

This gets to one notable critique of Open Theism presented by the Molinist, William Lane Craig. Craig argues that the God of Open Theism is "cognitively limited."[138] His argument is that even if God so chose to structure reality with contingent possibilities that don't become actualities until moral agents use their free will to choose them, why can't an infinitely intelligent God accurately predict the outcomes?

Maybe some of you have heard of the thought experiment commonly known as "Laplace's Demon" named after the 19th-century mathematician Pierre Simon Laplace. Laplace argued that if, hypothetically, there were somehow an intelligent being that knew the position of every atom in the universe at the present moment, and if that intelligence had enough computational power, it could calculate past movements and future trajectories of those atoms perfectly. So if God cannot perfectly predict the outcomes of all possibilities then either He doesn't have access to enough data or He has a limit on his computational power. Even if God structured reality to allow for the real choice between a pen and a stapler, couldn't He at least predict with one-hundred percent certainty which one you would choose? Suppose one says that God can perfectly predict with one hundred percent certainty the outcome of every possibility. In that case, we are back at believing something that doesn't seem different in any meaningful way from perfect foreknowledge.

Process theists have their beef with Open Theism too. After all, why does this all-good and all-loving God who is able to intervene and stop evil not do so every time...or at the very least, more often? They would argue that the open view only makes the problem of evil worse, because if God is capable of intervening to calm storms, heal lepers, and raise the dead but doesn't do it every time, then why doesn't He do it? It would seem like open theists are still stuck in the same position classical theists are when it comes to questions about why God doesn't stop evil and suffering if He's omnipotent enough to do so.

Finally, there's still that nagging question about who or

what tempted Satan to his primordial fall. Assuming, as Greg Boyd does, that Satan may have even filled the process of evolution with violence, predation, death, and disease, why did God allow Satan to have so much power and influence in the first place? If Satan has that much power and influence over the world, aren't we bordering dangerously close to making him like the Gnostics 'Demiurge that created the material world? It seems like God could still allow for free will with real possibilities but only allow different variations of good possibilities, like the freedom of the will to choose between having chocolate cake or chocolate chip cookies for dessert. Was the existence of Satan necessary to offer a choice between good and evil? Cause I really wish we were just choosing between cake and cookies with our free will.

$$* * *$$

This brings our tour into the 21st century. This has by no means been an exhaustive tour, and as I mentioned in the introduction, this tour has been devoid of women's voices. I could have given a chapter to someone like Sarah Coakley who is absolutely brilliant (and who I do discuss in the concluding chapters), but much of what I would be doing is restating updated arguments made by Thomas Aquinas and others in different ways. We have also, outside of Origen and Gregory of Nyssa, given virtually no attention to influential voices in the Christian East in the traditions of Eastern Orthodoxy and Coptic Christianity. I confess this was an act of intentional bias, not because the East is absent of brilliant theological voices, but because I know that most of my audience is situated in a Western context with church traditions most influenced by many of the names mentioned in this book.

I hope that thus far, my role as an impartial tour guide has somehow made you convinced of both the possible validity and, simultaneously, the deficiency of each perspective covered in each chapter. I want you to be able to respectfully assess the strengths and weaknesses of each without blindly consuming an Augustine, Luther, or Greg Boyd as gospel-truth or casually dismissing their arguments as trivial (or jumping to demonize any one of them as the bad guy that got it all wrong). If you are frustrated at this point and don't know what to think, that's okay too. This isn't supposed to be easy. If we're going to find a suitable framework, we need to stress test it before we accept it as true.

In these final chapters, I will share with you my conclusions about how I now make sense of the problem of evil and suffering. We'll review some of the key points in our journey, and I will extrapolate from them to build my own theodicy. While I welcome you to disagree with my conclusions, I encourage you to have a clear and coherent process for how you will sort out your conclusions on this subject. Hopefully, as I walk you through my conclusions, you can build a template from it for coming to your own.

PART IV- CONCLUSION

16. THE BIBLE, ORDER, NON-ORDER, & DISORDER

At this point in our journey, with so many options for Christians to choose how they will think about God, evil, and suffering, we may be tempted to remain permanently unsettled on the subject. Yet each of us has to act in the world in a particular way. We must pray in a particular way. We must interpret acts of evil and suffering in a particular way. How we act in the world is the most accurate reflection of what we *act*ually believe. My conclusions on this subject are not promised to be permanent. The cement can still be wet on them, but I have realized in the way that I pray, preach, and act in the face of perceived evils and suffering that I am living out some sort of theodicy. Far better to be intentional about sorting through what you believe now and if better evidence comes your way, update your beliefs and continue forward instead of never giving serious thought to the subject and potentially living under some oppressive deception (for example, like believing that God will only heal you if you hit some unknown minimum faith threshold).

In seeking a method for coming to some sort of conclusion on the problem of evil and suffering, I believe the place to begin is with the Bible. It's important to start here in any Christian theodicy because as a follower of Jesus I place a premium on the Scriptures that Jesus himself held to be authoritative, which include the Old Testament that Jesus read and prayed as inspired Scripture, as well as the New Testament canon that bears witness to the revelation of God in Christ Jesus. My goal then for interacting with those voices beyond the canon of Scripture is to see how their perspectives may shed light on what has been revealed in the biblical witness because it is in this biblical witness where we get closest to the historical witness and revelation of Jesus the Messiah.

As I do this, I must confess that I hold to several underlying philosophical and theological commitments. I presuppose a fundamentally good and intelligible reality even when I set out to understand God's self-disclosure in the language of the Scriptures. If that is not the case, then I have no foundation for trusting that the words on the page should even make sense. Some Christians can view the faculties of reason as being so broken that it would strip us of the ability to use it to even read the Bible. I find this low view of reason troubling as it makes both the Bible and the world we live in unintelligible. In consulting the biblical literature, I'm also affirming that God wants to be known, and in doing so I am confessing that I already believe in a God who acts imminently within His creation to reveal things about Himself and the world.

As we've observed in the early chapters of this book, there are some challenges in discerning a unified biblical theodicy in the pages of Scripture. If we read the Bible cover to cover, we would find what we should expect to find if God's revelation to humanity always happens in cultured communication and in particular cultural contexts- we should expect diversity of inspired expressions. As part of a diverse range of cultural expressions of God's revelation, we can see at times what appears to be diverse perspectives on the causality for various instances of evil and suffering within various books of the Bible. These are peoples who lived in various places, at various times, with various cultural customs, including the "scientific" and philosophical worldviews of their day. Could God have revealed to, say, the prophet Isaiah in the 8th century B.C., that humans one day would travel on rocket ships to the moon? It's doubtful that this kind of revelation could have happened between God and Isaiah because it would have made absolutely zero sense to someone living 2,700 years ago in the Ancient Near East.

No, God's revelation to the original biblical authors and audiences always works within their cultural framework. He uses their language, their symbols, their science, and oftentimes their philosophical worldview to disclose revelation that has important day-to-day, existential application within their imminent context but also has a transcendent trajectory that moves them gradually beyond their cultural limitations. This should help us make sense of the differences between the Old Testament, where there is no explicit mention of demons tormenting humanity with physical or psychological suffering, and the New Testament with its hundreds of mentions of demons, Satan, and principalities and powers.

This is why I believe that our earliest biblical books portray God as accepting more culpability for instances of immense suffering, with no competing spiritual forces like demons or Satan mentioned. In a cultural context where polytheism was the norm, Israel needed to learn the revelation of monotheism- a task that required the temporary elimination of any possible hint of competition or rivalry to Yahweh's will being accomplished in the world. As Israel began to see this truth, God slowly disclosed an increasing awareness of the existence of other spiritual principalities and powers, albeit spiritual entities who did not exist of their own will or accord, but were contingently existing because of God's intentional will, just like the rest of creation.

Historically, a quantum leap in this facet of God's revelation took place during the Second Temple period as we approached the birth of Christ. I believe this points to another insight into God's intentions with his progressive revelation. Not only did God refrain from disclosing malevolent spiritual entities called the "demonic" because of the need to pull Israel out of their polytheism, but I also believe God delayed properly disclosing the existence of these entities any earlier because, until Christ, humanity was virtually powerless to do anything about the demonic.

As a follower of Jesus, I have to take seriously, when considering the best possible explanations for evil and suffering, that the Jesus of the Gospels claimed that there was an evil "ruler of this world" (John 12:31). While that picture of demonic forces and Satan was not accessible to the original audience reading the book of Job with its picture of a "challenger angel" in God's divine court of angelic hosts, that revelation is accessible to us today.

Simultaneously, I do not believe that gives us the license to safely go back into the earlier revelations and force a new interpretation on those biblical texts. Can I go back and make the book of Exodus, which has no mention of Satan, be filled now with the activity of Satan in any instance of suffering just because it appears to be instances of suffering that are frequently attributed to Satan in the New Testament? No. Do the New Testament authors sometimes retroactively change the original meaning of texts within the Old Testament Scriptures? Yes. But neither you nor I should claim that level of authority. It is best to wrestle with the biblical revelation we have and not try to edit it. Where we feel the struggle and tension, we should accept our calling as the people grafted into that kingdom of priests named Israel - a name that means "one who struggles with God."

We must allow each book to speak on its own terms, and we must patiently work to step into its world and hear the inspired author's intended meaning. As we do this, I believe we'll find harmony in the revelations of the Scriptures, but we should not confuse harmony with a singular, univocal melody. Let the distinct notes of each biblical book remain distinct and not force them to communicate what other books of the Bible may communicate. Let's practice this now together using the book of Job once again as our starting point. What distinct notes from the book of Job may help us appreciate the broader symphony of

Scripture?

If we are building a theodicy from the Bible, there are several important revelations to emerge from the book of Job that we must account for:

1) Mesopotamian religion held that chaos, suffering, and evil were woven into the very fabric of the cosmos and even the gods were subject to them. Evil existed outside the jurisdiction of the gods. Job shows that this is not the case for the God of Israel. There are no forces beyond the jurisdiction of God. Chaos is not ontologically prior to God.

2) While the retribution principle or something akin to karma is often generally true, it is not a universal law that is always at work in every situation.

3) People do not always reap what they sow. People do not always get what they deserve. And you don't really want them to.

While in most cases we may be able to discern causal patterns for what sorts of actions produce pleasure and what sorts of actions produce suffering, the book of Job demonstrates that it is not universally true that a clearly discernible causal connection can be made between an action and a reaction. In more recent scientific history, we've learned this to be true at the quantum level with the discovery of quantum physics. There's so much more to the world than the Newtonian view of mechanical cause and effect. We see this in God's response to Job at the end of the book, where God essentially tells Job (and I'm obviously paraphrasing with great creative liberty), "Job, you're not going to be able to figure out all the causal connections in the universe here, buddy. Wait until you humans learn about quantum theory!"

Understanding that karma does not run the universe is

essential to building a biblically informed theodicy. God has seemingly structured reality in such a way that people often do not get what they deserve. I believe that we can see in the biblical narrative that God chose to create a reality where there is a degree of "will" or "potentiality" that we are free to wield for creative or destructive purposes. Why would God have built this kind of world versus another that might be devoid of such freedom of the will? I will address that at a later point.

In God's intentional designing of this kind of reality, He has provided a structure where mercy, grace, and forgiveness are possible; but in order for there to not be a rigid karmic structure that would eliminate the possibility of grace and forgiveness, God also needed to allow for the possibility that good people would not always get what they deserve either. Or, to put it another way- the possibility of mercy for one may require the possibility of the unjust suffering of another. We don't really want a world where people always get what they deserve, do we? If our answer is no and we don't want a world devoid of grace and mercy, then we may have to accept that unjust suffering for some may be a side effect of the kind of world where grace is possible. We can take heart that even those instances of unjust suffering will not continue on forever without a final setting right of all things.

When I was 19 years old, my former youth pastor died of cancer in his early 50s. He was a great man who was faithful to his wife, raised two wonderful daughters, volunteered as our youth pastor, and worked with special needs children for his full-time job. He never drank or smoked. He got up early every morning to go exercise before spending the rest of his day serving either special needs children or mentoring teenagers. I'd say he followed the wisdom of the book of Proverbs pretty well. Getting incurable cancer and dying was not getting what he deserved. (I know some who hold to some hyper-total depravity reading of Scripture may think, "well, we're all sinners deserving of death." To which I would kindly refer you to the responses of Job's friends who sound awfully similar and then ask you to see

God's response to Job's friends.)

Sitting beside him in hospice, with the shell of him that remained unable to recognize my face, I wondered how such a fate could befall this righteous man instead of some violent cartel leader or child brothel owner. But what if, in some sense, he was participating in the unjust sufferings of Christ? What if a world of grace and forgiveness, a world where bad people don't always get what they deserve, can't exist if all of the righteous get what they deserve? Maybe sometimes, that cup of unjust suffering just cannot pass from the righteous.

As I attempt to listen to the distinct notes of the book of Job inside the wider chorus of Scripture, I notice that the lynchpin of our faith rests on the fact that the cup of unjust suffering did not pass the only perfect righteous one- Jesus the Messiah, the lamb of God who takes away the sins of the world. The Cross unequivocally demonstrates that karma does not run the world. As the righteous Son of God suffers upon the Cross, He prays for forgiveness for the very ones who are murdering Him. Mercy is possible because God made a world where not everyone gets what they deserve, including the righteous.

This is not to say that all kinds of suffering are participating in Christ's suffering. In 1 Peter 4, the author writes, "But let none of you suffer as a murderer or a thief or an evildoer or as a meddler. Yet if anyone suffers as a Christian, let him not be ashamed, but let him glorify God in that name." There is undoubtedly suffering that we inflict on ourselves as the result of foolishness, but in places like the book of Job, Ecclesiastes, and ultimately on the Cross of Christ, we also see that not all suffering is the result of our sin or lack of wisdom.

This brings up an important opportunity for reflection on suffering and whether it is appropriate to always connect suffering with evil or whether Karth Barth had a valid insight about the shadowside of God's will. We most often associate suffering with experiences of physical or psychological pain, but whether we name an experience of displeasure or pain as an evil-induced experience of suffering or not is largely an act of perspectival interpretation. What if the forces of entropy and decay, the breaking down of our bodies as we age, and even physical death are experiences of suffering that may, in fact, be part of the good ordering of creation?

I remember a year or two ago, during a nice birthday dinner for my wife at a fancy restaurant, being hit with an epiphany. Together we felt the goodness of God all around us as we celebrated her life and our love together, and yet right in the middle of eating my steak, I had a sudden awareness of all the pain and possible suffering that went into the process of making this beautiful evening for my wife and me. I thought about the animals that died to become the food we were consuming, the hard work in the soil that someone gave to plant and grow the vines that produced the glass of wine we enjoyed, the aching feet of our waiter who was serving us, the cook in the kitchen who may have dreamed of doing something different with her life staving off her disappointment while she once again adjusts her mask during a pandemic, the truck driver who delivered the food and ingredients to the kitchen with a back that is aching from driving a semi-truck eight hours a day- all of it a sacrifice. On and on I could go, connecting all the dots to the human and non-human life that experienced some sort of discomfort, pain, decay, or destruction to make my beautiful "good" moment with my wife on her birthday possible.

Yes, I know what you're thinking-I definitely know how to turn a birthday party into a joyful celebration, don't I? You would have loved to see the look on my wife's face as I brought up the fact that the asteroid that collided with earth and killed off the dinosaurs some 65 million years ago making way for mammals like us to even occupy a place on the planet contributed to making our date so lovely. She thought that was wildly romantic of me.

Even the prevailing scientific theory for how our universe came to be some 14 billion years ago says that all of the matter and energy that exists in our universe was, at the very beginning, a single point. In some sense, it was the most ordered the universe could be with the lowest amount of possible entropy. When the Big Bang happened, all of that matter and energy moved from its initially ordered state to an ever-increasing expansion of entropy. Was that entropy evil? It seems that to claim that even entropy is evil is to go the way of the Gnostics, believing that something was fundamentally wrong with the material universe from the very moment it began. God's pronouncement of creation's fundamental goodness in Genesis 1 counters that notion.

The rightness of some kinds of sacrifice and death seems to be something that Jesus even affirms on some level, linking at least some types of natural decay and death to the Cross, when in John 12 He says, "The hour has come for the Son of Man to be glorified. Very truly I tell you, unless a kernel of wheat falls to the ground and dies, it remains only a single seed. But if it dies, it produces many seeds." When we take a moment to disengage from our screens or get outside the limits of our concrete city jungles and spend time on a farm or in a garden, we are quickly reminded of the necessary cycles of death and renewal in creation. This is literally happening every moment, all around us. It's not just the grain of wheat. Plants consume the sun's heat. Animals and humans consume the plants. Animals and humans consume other animals. When they die, the worms and soil consume their dead flesh and bones. Is this dis-ordered or rightly ordered? If it is all dis-ordered, then God is not very competent at His job as Creator.

Theologian Sarah Coakley and Christian philosopher Nancey Murphy have both argued similar points in the past.[139] There is a cruciform center to the patterns of death and renewal that we see in the natural world. There is altruistic behavior throughout the natural world that Coakley argues is as vitally important to a population's survival as the instincts of self-preservation. The kernel of wheat falling is not evil. The birthday dinner I had with my wife was not evil. Not all of these experiences of suffering are dis-ordered evil.

This is one of the problems with the problem of evil. Who gets to authoritatively interpret what is evil and what is good? When we play peekaboo with a baby, that baby's instinctive reaction to the event of us hiding our face is to interpret it in their limited cognitive abilities as an instance of us actually disappearing. Is that the true meaning of the event? Perhaps to the baby, but we in our superior abilities of rationality and wisdom know that we are not actually disappearing.

Are the entropic forces that set our galaxy into place evil? Is the grain of wheat falling to earth evil? Is the lactic acid build-up in my muscles as I try to power through one more push-up evil? No. Interpreting such events as evil would be the product of an immature or underdeveloped perspective on reality similar to the baby who thinks their parent's face disappears when they cover it.

Now, does this make evil purely a matter of perspectival interpretation? Should we accept all instances of suffering as a cup to be received? Should the abused wife continue to allow herself to suffer and simply change her perspectival interpretation of the event? Should those scientists searching for a cure to cancer stop their research and simply accept cancer as part of God's good creation? You can see the danger of a hyper-stoic acceptance of all events as opportunities for perspectival re-interpretation.

Just as we can see the difference between a game of peekaboo and something that could actually cause our face to disappear somehow, we should recognize the perspectival gap between our interpretive framing of the events of our world and that of an infinitely wise and intelligent God is all the more significant than the perspectival gap between an adult and an infant. The goal of event interpretation should be to expand our perspectives to increasingly interpret the world from the Gods-eye view.

If we are followers of Jesus who seek increasing conformity between our perspectives and His, then we should readily acknowledge from the ministry of Jesus that there are instances of suffering which are not part of the functional ordering of creation and do not fit into either the shadowside of creation or within the cruciform nature of reality. These are instances of genuine evil attributed to spiritual moral agents (such as Satan) or human moral agents, and in these cases of evil-induced suffering, we are called to resist the evil and bring remedy.

The Gospels are filled with these instances of evil-induced suffering and dis-order that Jesus resisted and alleviated, but for now, I will highlight just one example. Let's consider an incident of suffering and healing recorded in Luke 13. In this Gospel scene, Jesus says that this particular cripple woman has been bound by Satan for 18 years and then heals her. It is clear that Satan is a powerful spiritual moral agent who can inflict suffering and induce what we may label as a natural evil upon someone. The woman's ailment in Luke 13 was not a grain of wheat falling to the earth kind of suffering. It was a demonic attack. It was the product of a force of dis-order.

In each event of pain or suffering that appears to have a cause outside of the domain of our immediate control, it may be helpful to consider categorizing the cause of it into one of three possibilities:

1) Is this part of the **right-ordering** of creation that may be painful or uncomfortable, but not something to name as evil? (the rightly ordered, **cruciform nature of creation**)

2) Is this part of the **non-order** of creation (not dis-order) which humanity gets called as image bearers to transform from non-ordered chaos (but not malevolent) into something good and ordered?

3) Is this from a force of malevolent **dis-order** that is seeking to "steal, kill, and destroy"? (John 10:10)

So how do our interpretation of events ever come close to accurately naming from a God's-eye view a particular instance of suffering as being part of either the uncomfortable right-ordering of creation, the result of non-ordered forces we are called to bring good ordering to, or a work of malevolent disorder that we should actively resist, work to prevent, and bring healing to?

Because when it comes down to it, all of our efforts to sift through all this philosophy and theology should be driven by the more fundamental desire to find a proper existential application that helps us know how to respond to the disruptions of suffering in our real life. Suffering will not cause a collapse of our meaning-making structures and create in us an existential crisis of faith if we can find a meaning and an appropriate response to the suffering. Can we transition from being the baby playing peekaboo to being a maturing adult with an ever-increasing expansion of perspective, growing in our ability to discern and be conformed to the God's-eye view? Yes, and we can do this while affirming with the Apostle Paul that in this age, we all will see only in part.

> *"For we know in part and we prophesy in part, but when completeness comes, what is in part disappears. When I was a child, I talked like a child, I thought like a child, I reasoned like a child. When I became a man, I put the ways of childhood behind me. For now we see only a reflection as in a mirror; then we shall see face to face. Now I know in part; then I shall know fully, even as I am fully known."*
> 1 Corinthians 13:9-12

Because we see in a mirror dimly even as we earnestly search the Scriptures, it is important that we compare what we see in that mirror with what others before us have claimed to see in that mirror. This is why we took so much time to comb through the perspectives of some of history's most influential Christian minds. We want to compare and contrast what we see in part so that we may see the whole more clearly. Where did you see harmonious pictures? Where did you notice sharp dissonance between the Scriptures and other voices? Allow me to show you the picture I have built with the help of some of the key Christian voices of the past that we have already explored together.

17. MY SYNTHESIS OF PAST PERSPECTIVES

From the very beginning of Christian history, we see that the earliest Christians continued with the New Testament tradition of assigning blame to Satan for the instances of malevolent dis-order that they saw in the world. Ignatius, in the first and early second century, saw instances of individual sin, disruption of Christian community, heresy, and blasphemy as Satanic attempts to sow dis-order and dysfunction in the world, yet Christ's power was above and beyond the wiles of the Devil and Christians can resist those forces of dis-order.

Polycarp of Smyrna (88-156 AD), a disciple of John, saw false teaching and the rejection of the Cross as part of the malevolent dis-order of Satan, but Polycarp did not see all suffering as evil to be resisted. He also saw his own martyrdom as sharing in the cup of Christ. His famous last words were, "I bless you Father for judging me worthy of this hour, so that in the company of the martyrs I may share the cup of Christ." For Polycarp, all things in heaven and earth were subject to Christ, and even his own participation in cruciform suffering was not purely an act of malevolent disorder from the deceived Roman powers, but rather it was part of the Father's right-ordering that would produce good fruit in the world.

In the second century, Justin Martyr saw malevolent

satanic dis-order at work in the heretical deceptions of the Gnostics and Marcionites. For Justin, the possibility for dis-order to exist comes as a logical side effect of God's allowance for moral agents to exercise a degree of free will. Yet Justin is clear that no moral agent, spiritual or human, can ultimately usurp the will and purposes of God. God's delay in the final cessation of all dis-order is because God desires the maximum number of human beings to experience His goodness and forgiveness. The possibility that more humans who have yet to be born can eventually share in His goodness outweighs the side effects of allowing for the continued presence of malevolent dis-order.

Irenaeus (135-202 AD) believed that it was in God's original good intention and right-ordering of creation for humanity to undergo a maturation process that includes pain and suffering. The process of moving from being like children into an increasing state of perfection is all part of God's good plan. This does not discount that there are forces of malevolent dis-order (specifically Satan) at work in creation that we must resist. But because humanity consistently fails at resisting the temptation towards this dis-order, Jesus comes as true God and true man. Through a process called "recapitulation," He undoes humanity's sins and Satan's dis-order.

Through these first two to three centuries of Christian theology, there is an unequivocal and consistent witness about a cosmic conflict at work in creation. This, again, is what I have called *moderate cosmic dualism*. It is the cosmic dualism that I believe we find in the New Testament and in the early Church Fathers, and it is squarely situated between a monistic theodicy that sees all instances of suffering, even the events that some may find to be the most egregious instances of evil, as flowing from the unfettered will of God, and a radical ontological dualism like that of the Gnostics who saw creation as filled with so much dis-order that it had to be, on an ontological level, the product of either some flawed or sinister demiurge.

Monistic theodicies are forced to interpret all events as being ultimately right-ordered logically, and radical ontological dualists are forced to place a disproportionate and ultimately unbiblical amount of weight on creation being dis-ordered. The existential pitfalls of each are that, on the one hand, if one over-interprets all instances of suffering as being right-ordered, they will miss out on the opportunity to fulfill part of their human vocation as image bearers called to bring right-ordering to non-order. Not only that, but they will continue to allow instances of injustice and dysfunction to be continually perpetuated, especially among the poor or oppressed who may be disproportionately affected as victims of these cycles of dis-order.

Some historical examples of those that I believe edge too close to a monistic theodicy and thereby overinterpret instances of suffering as being right-ordered are Augustine (post-Pelagian controversy), Martin Luther, and John Calvin. Some may also see the metaphysics of Thomas Aquinas as inevitably leading to a monistic theodicy, but this is a point of debate in which I tend to see Aquinas somewhere between a monistic theodicy and a moderate cosmic dualism that defends the validity of free will. Those historical figures or movements that I would see as hyper-monistic in their theodicy would include the Deists, Friedrich Schleiermacher, and John Piper as one popular contemporary example.

There is certainly a danger if one moves into the opposite theodicy ditch. Veer too far in the other direction into radical ontological dualism like the Gnostics and you may find yourself in a constant state of anxiety about the amount of perceived evil in the world and crippled by an inability to have any logical basis for assurance that God can, and will, triumph over all the evil. On top of all that, if the state of the material universe is so corrupted and fallen, you lose all basis for trusting reason or your experiences. This calls into question all great disciplines of general revelation like math or science.

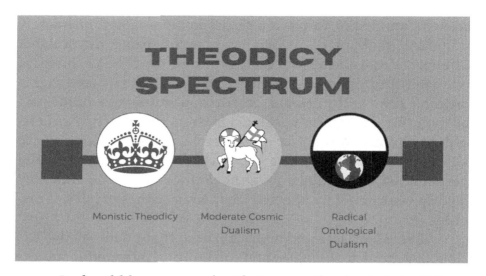

THEODICY SPECTRUM

Monistic Theodicy   Moderate Cosmic   Radical
                        Dualism   Ontological
                                          Dualism

It should be no surprise that some theological traditions that teeter on radical ontological dualism produce some of the strongest conspiracy cultures. After all, if dis-order rivals God's right-ordering of creation to this extent, then it's internally consistent in that interpretive framework to be concerned that a credit card or vaccine might be the mark of the beast. These kinds of gnostic ontological mythologies see all of reality as a conspiracy.

As cognitive scientist John Vervaeke points out in his *Awakening from The Meaning Crisis* lecture series, the Nazis may have been the ultimate manifestation of a gnostic mythological narrative in a historic human civilization.[140] To Hitler, the whole world was dominated by an evil that Germans must struggle against, defeat, and overcome. The Jews and their God were the evil gatekeepers to be defeated and destroyed. Every instance of human sickness or disability was something to be eradicated from the earth through eugenics and the state-sponsored mating of the *lebensborn*, who the Nazis saw as the genetically ideal humans called to eventually repopulate the entire earth.

This is the genuine danger of theodicies that move from a moderate cosmic dualism into hyper-dualism and become held by a people at a culture-wide level. If all of reality is a struggle between good and evil, and if you divide the world into teams of light and dark, your disposition towards others outside of your cultural tribe will be one of suspicion, fear, and hate. Now I want to be clear that not all of the people who have held to a more ontologically dualist theodicy turn out to be Nazis or bad people. For example, I do think in some ways that Greg Boyd's "warfare worldview" theodicy veers too closely to ontological dualism, yet he is committed to non-violence and really dislikes Nazis (sidenote: Boyd's position is still probably closer to the early Church Fathers on the theodicy spectrum chart than many of his detractors like to admit). In bringing up these potential pitfalls, I'm not trying to commit a slippery slope fallacy or build a straw man; instead, I merely want to offer a concrete example of the day-to-day implications of how bad theology and theodicy can play out in the world in disastrous ways.

Historically, some of the theologians or groups that I believe have veered too closely to a radical ontological dualism or have been explicitly hyper-dualist in their theodicy have included: the Manicheans, the Gnostics, Marcion, Origen, some Pietist movements, some expressions of Liberation theology, Process Theism, and Open Theism.

The moderate cosmic dualism of the New Testament and early Church Fathers takes seriously the forces of malevolent dis-order but acknowledges that this struggle has been allowed in the arena of creation by the intentional will of God. Some of these Church Fathers took the cosmic struggle of the New Testament so seriously that they came up with cosmological backstories for things like the fall of Satan, which admittedly were pretty unfounded in the biblical revelation. Some of these theories, such as Tertullian's proposal in the third century that Satan was once the wisest of the angels but became jealous of humanity's special relationship with God and led a rebellion against God, are interesting speculations that many people still believe today, but because they are not explicitly revealed in the Scriptures, I see no reason to accept them. Where Scripture is silent, it's okay to be silent.

I believe we also see in these early Church Fathers a propensity to see instances of suffering as either opportunities to participate in Christ's suffering as part of the cruciform intentions of God's right-ordering of creation or as part of the satanic dis-order that flows from the misuse of the will. To these ancient thinkers, what we'd be apt to label as the "natural" world was far more influenced by the will of agentic "spiritual" forces of good and evil than people in the post-Newtonian world of the West are comfortable with. The ancients left little room for more "mindless" non-ordered forces to exist. Even though we find in the cultural context of the book of Job that those ancient near eastern mythologies had morally-neutral, non-ordered chaos creatures like Leviathan, they would not have understood something like "gravity" to be a law that simply is and has no will or goals to it.

The symbolic affirmation of forces of Leviathan-like non-order in the special revelation of the Bible and the light of general revelation in the sciences, which afford us so many accurate insights into the workings of the material world, lead me to believe that there are, in fact, many events in the world that are happening that are not directly the product of any agentic causality other than God's will to create and sustain those processes that operate in the arena of creation. While the Newtonian understanding of the universe as a machine certainly had its drawbacks, it has also helped us understand causal patterns and develop appropriate responses that have vastly improved the quality of life on this planet. Understanding that there are "mindless" processes in the machinery of our universe that are not conscious agents with a will for good or evil is a necessary perspective to help us properly interpret the events of the world around us.

In God's vocational calling of the human species in Genesis 1, we see God call humanity to act in God's likeness and bring right-ordering to the non-moral life of the natural world. Anyone who's worked to bring some functional good-ordering out of an interaction with plant life, animal life, or the non-agentic forces of nature knows this sort of work is not always filled with immediate gratification or pleasure. I live in Minnesota where we can go for entire months in the winter not making it above freezing. Every time I step outside on those days, I experience a degree of suffering. Tempted as I am to see this kind of Minnesota weather as a Satanic attack, it simply isn't. It's just weather.

What is the right interpretative framework to employ when a brutal Minnesota winter storm comes my way? Do I try to cast out a demon, or do I bundle up, grab a sled, and transform a potential instance of non-ordered suffering into a rightly-ordered moment of joy sledding with my kids? All of the homes we live in exist as a transformation of the natural world (the wood, the brick, the concrete used to construct it, etc) to shield us from not only the forces of dis-order, such as a burglar who may try to steal from us, but primarily from the sometimes chaotic, non-ordered forces in creation that could cause us harm. A winter storm isn't evil; it's a mindless process built into the functionality of the whole system. Being called in the likeness of God, humans can see this as an opportunity to transform chaos into order. We are invited to partner with God in bringing order out of chaos.

We build levees and dams to control raging waters. We extract materials out of fossils that power our cars and keep us warm in the cold. We carve paths in the wilderness so that people can hike and more easily enjoy the natural beauty of creation. In every encounter with non-order there is the potential for it to become right-ordered or dis-ordered. Some of the great Christian thinkers of the third through fifth centuries have helped us to understand this.

Adapting some of the language and "science" of their day, Origen, Gregory of Nyssa, and Augustine used the ideas of Plato and Plotinus to relevantly communicate many truths of the biblical revelation into their cultural context. While I have sharp disagreements with each of them on at least several points, I find that their understanding of what evil is to be profoundly helpful in shaping my own theodicy. What Origin, Gregory of Nyssa, and Augustine all agree upon is that evil is not a metaphysical necessity on par with the Good.

God is the absolute source of the good, the true, and the beautiful and is the ground of all being. God is pure actuality, but contingent moral beings contain potentiality. Using our potentiality to move away from the Good (which is God) is evil because to move away from the Good is to head into increasing states of dis-order, the end of which would be non-being itself. The use of our will and potentiality to move towards the Good in ever-increasing union with God is the correct and proper use of our will. Evil then is the dysfunction and dis-order that emerges from the misused will.

In the arena of God's creation, there are various moral agents with wills that possess varying degrees of freedom. Satan and the demonic are real spiritual moral agents who have misused their will. The scope of the potential uses for their will may include affecting creation in ways that are much different than the ways human agents impact the world. This affirmation is in keeping with the biblical picture of Satan and the demonic influencing some natural evils such as instances of sickness and physical ailments.

Of the three, I may be most fond of Gregory of Nyssa. I appreciate that he did not claim to know the cosmological backstory that led to the fall of those spiritual agents, but still offers humble speculation that Satan was the first moral agent in creation to "close his eyes to the Good." Thinking of evil as the misuse of our potential is incredibly helpful as one considers that the consistent hope of salvation in the New Testament is not merely the avoidance of judgment but the positive reward of union with God (2 Peter 1:4).

Through the finite symbols and lesser goods of creation, we get glimpses of the Good as invitations to celebrate that goodness and to hear the beckoned calls of the transcendent God drawing us onward in our journey beyond the finite good to the infinite Good. The misuse of our potentiality to either settle for the glimpse of the Good we find in the finite symbol, that momentary sliver of beauty we experience in a finite created thing, and to name it as the chief end of all our aims, or to pervert the Good into a tool that we believe can elevate ourselves to the throne of God - this is the evil misuse of the intended right-ordering of creation. This is the dis-order that Gregory calls "the retrocession of the soul from the Beautiful."

Up until the later years of Augustine's life, we had seen unanimous consent among Christian writers on the genuine potentiality in the human will to respond to God's love positively or to misuse the will for sin and dis-order. The post-Pelagian-controversy version of Augustine popularized the idea that the will does not possess the capability to respond positively to God. Augustine's emphasis on the need for Christ and the regeneration of the Spirit for salvation were important points but presented an unnecessary wedge between God's grace and human free will. Prior Church Fathers had rightly understood that it is always God's grace that precedes any movement of the will toward God. Their affirmation of the ability of the will to respond positively to God's grace was not a claim that the will was responsible for mustering up its own salvation. Instead, it was an affirmation of the genuine culpability of those wills that would reject God's grace, love, and mercy.

This is an important point of practical methodology when doing theology. If we find a fairly consistent chain of agreement on a particular subject from the Apostles through the first few successive generations of Christian history but then note a deviation from what came before, that deviation isn't automatically wrong, but it should be a red flag for concern or further inspection. The Eastern Orthodox theologian and philosopher David Bentley Hart has argued that Augustine's misunderstanding of the nature of grace and human will, commonly called "total depravity" in Protestant circles, may stem from Augustine having engaged with a "misleading" Latin translation of Romans and an educational deficiency in his ability to properly engage with the original Greek text. [141] It's an interesting theory, and one that is not without its pushback, but as one can't help but note the difference in Augustine's theology on this point from his predecessors, we are left to wonder, "why the change?" Augustine's influence on future generations of Lutherans, Calvinists, and other Reformed groups is undeniable. If one is inclined to believe that ideas like total depravity, double predestination, or that infants who die without being baptized experience eternal damnation only worsen the problem of evil, their challenge should be levied at Augustine before any later Protestant theologian.

The only comparable influence on Christian theology to Augustine is Thomas Aquinas. Encountering the work of Aquinas helped rescue me from a hidden Gnosticism that had been a part of my younger Charismatic-Evangelical experience. In the particular Christian contexts I inhabited for most of my early life, the world was primarily an evil place that we looked forward to escaping either in a *Left Behind* style rapture or when we died through a soul-escape to the postmortem retirement resort we called heaven. Mainstream science was run by a cabal of atheist scientists hellbent on eradicating Christianity. There was no goodness in human reasoning until, perhaps, after one got saved. I'm being a bit hyperbolic here, but some of you might be laughing because you know your own experience wasn't that far removed from this description.

Aquinas 'affirmation of the goodness of the material world and the God-given value of reason and sense experience changed my life and opened me up to what the Apostle Paul argued in Romans 1. God made "plain" in His creation his "eternal power and divine nature." Natural theology is biblical. Science and faith aren't at odds. All truth is God's truth. Once again, the importance of Aquinas 'theological contribution to the foundations of the future Scientific Revolution can't be overstated. God isn't tricking us when we study the world and rightly employ our faculties of reason to discern causal patterns. It's God's gift of common grace to all, and it's a gift that has alleviated the suffering of billions through the scientific and medicinal advancements which have brought so much right-ordering to both non-order and dis-order.

Aquinas 'theology also gives us an essential categorical distinction between God as a primary cause and God as a secondary cause in the events of the world. God is the primary cause of all that exists, not just as the first cause that started it all, but as that which actively holds and sustains all things. God can will that all things exist at this moment while allowing for degrees of autonomy in those things He sustains. This allows for the existence of natural disasters or wars that God is not specifically willing to happen as the direct or secondary cause. Again, this framework from Aquinas gives us room to see that categories like *non-order* exist as potential invitations from God to us to participate in what is sometimes called "the cultural mandate" (or dominion mandate) located in Genesis 1:26-30. Aquinas even specifically affirms that some of the non-ordered suffering we see in the natural world is just what happens when you have a creator-creature distinction. Though Aquinas lived long before Darwin, Thomistic theology hasn't been shaken by the 19th-century revelation of a long history of decay and predation in the plant and animal world either.

From the work of Luther and subsequent generations of Christian thinkers who emphasized the role of suprarational faith in rightly knowing God, we can preserve the call to trust God even when we cannot rationally figure out His ways from our experiences with the natural world. While we should wholeheartedly affirm the Romans 1 foundation for natural theology, we must also hold our regard for reason and science in tension with another claim from the Apostle Paul. The "message of the Cross is foolishness to those who are perishing" and the "intelligence of the intelligent" is "frustrated" by God's self-disclosure in a crucified Jewish peasant (1 Cor. 1:17-19).

There is often a very real sense in our experiences of

suffering that God is hidden from us. Luther encourages us to consider that, paradoxically, it is in this sensation of hiddenness that God may be most found. Our perception of God's absence does not indicate a genuine absence on God's part. The Cross appeared to be the utter failure of God, a complete hiddenness of His goodness, and an abandonment of his Messiah in that moment, and yet to the Apostle Paul it is the wisdom of God.

Sure, Luther presents many ideas about God and evil that I find inconsistent with the biblical witness and the earliest Christian voices. I have no problem setting those aside while retaining the good of what Luther and Calvin had to say. In the case of Calvin, I sometimes wonder if what I perceive as his theological shortcomings stem from the fact that he attempted to systematize a cohesive theological system in a way that simply went too far and flattened the diversity of the Scriptures into a singular monovocal melody. For example, if one starts with Calvin's view of divine sovereignty and predestination as the starting point, then the idea that God has predestined to only save some and to deem others as vessels of dishonor is internally coherent. While it is internally coherent as a systematic theology, I personally do not find it consistent with the biblical witness, nor do I find it to be a viable solution for the problem of evil. Yet, I gladly worship regularly with Calvinist brothers and sisters in Christ and am so deeply thankful for the many ways that Calvinist and Reformed thinkers have made me a better follower of Jesus.

Calvin does provoke us to consider that often oversimplified solutions presented to the problem of evil such as, "well, God gave us free will..." or "it's actually Satan who's responsible for evil" aren't as bulletproof as some think they are. Why did God allow for the potentiality of evil at all? Did it surprise Him? Was He just incompetent at designing the cosmos? Did He intentionally allow it? What's the difference between intentionally allowing it and predestining it? For Calvin, the buck starts and stops with God's sovereignty. This can be a great consolation to many. To think that God has some genuine rival thwarting His will undercuts His omnipotence and may fill some with anxiety and fear. If there's one thing you can count on from Calvin and his followers, it's that they aren't ever going to fall for Gnosticism.

18. DIS-ORDER & THE MOST BEAUTIFUL OF ALL POSSIBLE SONGS

Marvel's *WandaVision* is a story about the magically gifted Wanda Maximoff (AKA the Scarlet Witch) who creates an alternate reality bubble in the fictional town of Westview. In episode 5 of the series, Wanda's superpowered-synthezoid-lover Vision voyages to the outskirts of town and pushes himself beyond the bounds of the alternate reality bubble spread like a canopy over the city. As he moves from the center of the town to beyond the bounds of Westview, he begins to disintegrate into non-existence. What we find out is that this particular version of Vision was completely contingent on Wanda's willful sustaining of the alternate reality bubble. As he moved away from his source of life, he discovered that his existence was contingent on living in the magic canopy that Wanda had created.

If we conceive of all contingent reality that God made and sustains being like the magic reality bubble Wanda made in *WandaVision* (except with our reality being good!) and if we think of evil as a movement away from the center of this town and beyond the boundaries of the bubble into non-existence, we are left with a question: why would a perfectly good and all-powerful God allow for any possible movement away from the Good at all?

Unless we go the route of the radical ontological dualists, we must confess that God intentionally allowed for the potentiality of dis-order in His creation. The radical ontological dualists will suggest that there is some kind of force or being metaphysically prior or equal to God's will. For some process theists, it is "creativity." The contemporary "open and relational" Christian philosopher Thomas Jay Oord argues that "love" is metaphysically prior or superior to "will" in God.[142] I can see some of the existential and emotional appeals of these theodicies, because some may feel that this somehow absolves God of the responsibility for the horrific things they may have endured. The cost of believing such a theodicy is too great for me.

These theodicies reduce God to being just another agent in the creation-arena whose will is subject to wills beyond his own. If that is the case, then we can have little certainty that the will that holds all things together in creation at this very moment will be able to continue to hold it in the next. Could we wake up tomorrow and all the laws of physics be usurped by utter chaos and absurdity? If something else is metaphysically prior or superior to God's will, then that awful outcome is entirely possible...dare, even likely.

Along with Origen, Gregory of Nyssa, Augustine, Aquinas, Luis de Molina, and Gottfried Leibniz, I believe that in order for there to be a creator-creation distinction, God would need to allow for a creation with potentiality. This creation has the potentiality to move away from the Good; without that potentiality to move away from the Good there would be only the Good. The Good as pure actuality with no potentiality to be anything other than the Good is God, and God cannot make God. What we can trust as we understand the logical (and biblical) necessity of God as the highest good, is that even in God's willful creation of a reality with the potentiality for movement away from Himself, God's infinite intelligence brought into existence the best of all possible worlds.

Now, I know the language of "best of all possible worlds" is not without its dissenters, but before I give my own nuanced defense of it (and along with it, my response to the question of "why did God allow for any potential dis-order?"), we have to address some of the relevant questions about God's relation to time and the nature of God's knowledge as the transcendent ground of all existence.

Frankly, I don't have the slightest clue how the physics of time works beyond our experience of it. I'd be lying if I said I comprehended Einstein's theory of general relativity, other than it making for a cool plot device in Christopher Nolan's film *Interstellar*. I'm not a physicist. Even if I was, understanding God's relationship to time might just be a category of knowledge in that Kantian "noumenal" plane that may simply be beyond the bounds of rational deduction or empirical observation. The classical theist and the process theist can have their speculative debates about the nature of God's relationship to time and process, but no matter what philosophical camp you land in, there must be two biblical affirmations that we hold to and subordinate our philosophical speculations under.

First, time cannot be a metaphysical power above and beyond God otherwise it would be God. Secondly, God is a *living God* with real relationship to time-bound creatures. He not only constructs and sustains the creation-arena, but He also acts in the creation-arena as an agent. These affirmations are part of the historic Christian affirmation that God is both transcendent and immanent.

The classical theist may struggle to find ways of genuinely affirming the immanence of God acting in real relation to time-bound creatures, while the process theist may struggle to truly affirm the transcendence of God and not merely conceive of Him as an agent acting in a pre-existing arena (pre-existing by who/what other will? Creativity? Love?). God, by definition, is that which is necessary for there to be anything at all, and therefore, by definition, God must be supremely transcendent.

If God is transcendent and the ground of all that exists,

then there can be no limitations on what is known to God. Now the open theist may agree with this but prefer to say that the kind of reality that God has structured contains possibilities that have unknowable outcomes until a moral agent uses their free will (aka, their potentiality) to choose to make that potentiality an actuality. For years, I considered this to be a powerful argument and was a card-carrying open theist. I still believe that there's plenty of biblical warrant for taking open theism seriously and think it's unnecessary to have evangelical inquisitions where we lob charges of heresy against the Clark Pinnocks and Greg Boyds of the world; but ultimately, I am no longer convinced by the argument.

For reasons I have brought up in public conversation with Greg Boyd on two different occasions, the problem I see is that even if God somehow structured reality in the way that open theists describe, the nature of God's transcendent being- which has not only created every molecule in the universe but presently upholds and sustains their very existence- means that the position of every molecule in the universe and every neuron firing in your brain is presently known to God. If the location of everything is presently known to God and God has no limitations to His cognitive "computing" powers, then even if He so chose to build real possibilities into the very structure of the creation-arena, He should be able to predict every single molecules trajectory and every single neural network connection in our brain that will happen in this next moment. Not only that, but He would be able to predict with complete certainty the outcome of every single moment that would follow thereafter. If not, then God would have some computational limitations that make Him inferior to even Laplace's Demon.

This is the best possible world. Aquinas, Molina, Leibniz, and others who believed that this reality is the best possible reality for God to have made were correct. Fully comprehending that this kind of creation-arena filled with moral agents that possess potentiality would lead to movements away from the

Good, God still brought this reality to be. Why? Why would God still create a world that allows for the possibility of evil? There are two reasons.

The first reason is that the weight of the goodness, truth, and beauty in the sum total of all creation, in every moment and in the glory to come, is so far beyond even the worst conceivable instances of suffering. It is better for this world to exist than to not exist. Could we ever assess the total amount of goodness or evil in the universe and come to an objective conclusion on which there is more of in any given moment? The task is humanly impossible. If the task is impossible, then how could we say confidently, "I know God could have brought about a better world than this"?

Let's play with Molina's theory a bit and assume for a moment that somehow logically or temporally prior to the *in the beginning* God pulls a Dr. Strange in *Avengers: Infinity War* and runs simulations on 14,000,000,605 possible outcomes for the story of creation, factoring the innumerable ways every human and angelic agent may use the potentiality of their will. Which one will He decide to actualize? If it's not the best story, then why? What stopped God from bringing about the best possible story? I don't see the need to choose between limiting God's competency or His goodness. If He is all-powerful and all-good, then this must be the best possible story.

All of these analogies are ultimately insufficient. Comparing God to a magic Marvel superhero-wizard and speaking about God running mental simulations or making computations is obviously language that does not capture what the Infinite Ground of All Existence is. However, even these limited analogies should cause us to pause and consider what is possible for the infinite God. If God's wisdom is undoubtedly beyond Dr. Strange's time-stone magic trick and God's goodness is the source of all virtues that our heroes, both real and fictitious, participate in in-part, then the world that God brought to be must be the best possible world.

Does this mean that the world we have has been

fated to be this way? Doesn't this ultimately absolve humans of responsibility for their moral choices? Doesn't God's foreknowledge functionally mean God's foreordaining? Many brilliant Christian minds from Thomas Aquinas to C.S. Lewis didn't think so. Because God built potentiality into the creation-arena, we possess the moral capacity to use our will to move away from the Good or toward the Good in an ongoing development of *caritas*. To Aquinas, *caritas* was the highest virtue- a manifestation of the selfless love of God brought about by the indwelling empowerment of the Spirit.

God is the primary cause of all things as Ultimate Reality, the transcendent ground of all being, and the willful sustainer of every moment in the creation-arena, but He is not the acting agent or secondary cause of all things in the creation-arena. Some will ask the question, "Well, how can this be if He can perfectly foreknow or predict how all things will come to be?" This is where I must confess a degree of mystery between these core affirmations of God's transcendent sovereignty and human moral responsibility. The open theists were right to say that the biblical narrative becomes nonsensical if human moral responsibility is just illusory. Aquinas knew this to be true too. Some like Luther and Calvin went too far in imposing some of the possible implications of God's transcendence upon the biblical revelation of human moral responsibility.

Some may see all appeals to mystery as a way of turning a blind eye away from a logical inconsistency or just a byproduct of intellectual slothfulness, but as we have seen throughout this series, all theodicies eventually get to a point of mystery. If Kant was right about our epistemological limitations as humans (and I think he was on to something), then mystery is an inevitable feature of the human experience. God is transcendent. God is imminent. We are responsible for our actions. I simply cannot throw out any of these three affirmations even if I can't find a perfect philosophical container to make them all play neatly together within.

The second reason I believe that God allowed for the

potentiality of evil in this world is related to Origen's theory that our present age functions as a school and hospital for our souls- albeit without Origen's insistence on the inherent immortality of the soul. God in Christ, having both a divine nature and a human nature, is transforming human nature and will continue to heal our natures until we get to the point where we only use our potentiality to will the Good. We often shiver in repulsion when we look back at the horrors of history and wonder, "how could a person ever have done that?"   For example, consider the Nazi eugenics movement. While it is not impossible for such a movement to happen again, the overwhelming moral consensus of humanity across the globe would now be to name as evil any attempt at recreating the Nazi eugenics experiments. As historian Tom Holland highlights in *Dominion: How the Christian Revolution Remade the World,* the ethical compass that emerges out of the Christian story and Christian community has completely changed humanity's understanding of right and wrong. Human nature is changing.

Through eons of human experience with the dis-ordered nature of sin and through the compelling beauty of Christ transforming humanity, human nature is slowly learning, healing, and being transformed. The transformation will be so complete that when we get to the Age to Come, our desire for even the tiniest of sins will be as strong as your present desire to punch a baby in the face. Though you have it within your potential ability to hit a baby, your will has no desire to use its potentiality that way. So it will be with every possible temptation and vice toward dis-order. Our potentiality will remain, but our human nature will be like Christ's and will operate in perfect, indissoluble union with the Father's will.

One need not believe in the same metaphysical claims as Origen to believe that God has remedial and rehabilitative purposes for this present age. We need not confuse a historic Christian eschatological vision of the promised culmination of God's renewing work in the Age to Come with the misguided contemporary myth of human progress persisting in one continuous straight line of moral and technological improvement either. The Christian hope isn't unfettered "progress," but the promise that as surely as Christ rose, we can trust that "he who began a good work in you will carry it on to completion" (Philippians 1:6). We are undergoing a metamorphosis from the nature of the first Adam to a truer and better human nature in the Second Adam, Jesus Christ. "But we know that when Christ appears, we shall be like him, for we shall see him as he is" (1 John 3:2b).

Even after this long journey together, the lingering question may still remain- why bring about creation at all if the capacity for so much evil is even a possibility? Thus far we have primarily grappled with philosophical or theological reasons as we've searched for answers, but perhaps when considering why God chose to bring about this kind of world we should also consider *aesthetic* reasons. What role does beauty play in God's purposes? Here's where the work of an author not known as a theologian but as a literary master of poetic fiction and fantasy may yield one of the most helpful theodicies.

J.R.R. Tolkien was a 20th-century English writer and professor best known for creating the fantasy works of *The Hobbit* and *The Lord of the Rings*, but it is in Tolkien's lesser known, posthumously published work *The Silmarillion* that Tolkien most explicitly draws upon his Christian faith to compose a cosmological back-story for Middle Earth. Though there is no explicit backstory for an event many would call the "fall of Satan" in the biblical literature, Tolkien's fictional creation myth has clear points of connection to long-held theories among Christians about the fall of Satan (most notably those of John Milton's *Paradise Lost*). Though fictitious, the symbolic mythology of Tolkien's creation myth is filled with rich theological truths and even a profound defense for God's designing of a creation with the potentiality for dis-ordered evil.

In the "Ainulindalë" (the opening creation account of *The Silmarillion*), Eru Iluvatar (the name for God in this fantasy epic) as his first act of creation brings about the Ainur, which are the spiritual moral agents of Tolkien's universe. God teaches these angelic spirits music so that they would all participate in God's great symphony. Each is given the potentiality of voicing their own notes in the song of creation, but the music they create only finds its right-ordering by playing and singing in harmony with God's beautiful symphony. They are free to truly act as sub-creators improvising notes and creatively expressing in song the fire that God put within them, as long as the music they make is in harmony with the theme God as the composer has instructed them to play within.

For those of you who are musicians, you could almost conceive of this as a jazz or blues jam session where experienced musicians know how to play together to make one cohesive song even though the individual notes are not rigidly prescribed to each player. As a guitarist, I know that if I sit in on a blues jam all I need to know is the musical key we're playing in, and I can jump in and contribute with even the most basic of minor pentatonic scale improvisation. Well, one of these angelic-like spirits named *Melkor* is the first Ainur to use his potentiality to make music that is not in harmony with creation's song. Melkor is clearly the Satan figure in this story. If you imagine this as an A minor blues shuffle, it was like Melkor started shredding in E flat and kept changing time signatures like it's a Mars Volta prog-rock song.

This Satan-like Melkor attempts to bring dis-order into the music. Why? We don't know, just as we have no real idea what tempted the original Tempter in our true creation story. Certainly, there's vanity at play in Melkor's discordant song. He's a musical virtuoso, and like many musical virtuosos, he wants to break free from the band that he believes is holding him back from his proper place in the spotlight. Before long, other Ainur break away from the great symphony of creation and join

Melkor in trying to make their own song, but as this happens, it becomes apparent that this new discordant song is far less beautiful. Like the guitar player who knows all of his scales but just won't stop soloing, Melkor and the other rebelling angelic Ainur have used their potentiality to make a much less beautiful song.

But here's where the brilliance of Tolkien's creation myth shines brightly, not only as a theological parable but also as a compelling theodicy. As God moves the song of creation into its third movement, Tolkien writes:

> Then again Ilúvatar [God] arose, and the Ainur perceived that his countenance was stern; and he lifted up his right hand, and behold, a third theme grew amid the confusion, and it was unlike the others. For it seemed at first soft and sweet, a mere rippling of gentle sounds in delicate melodies; but it could not be quenched, and it took to itself power and profundity. And it seemed at last that there were two musics progressing at one time before the seat of Ilúvatar, and they were utterly at variance.
>
> The one was deep and wide and beautiful, but slow and blended with an immeasurable sorrow, from which its beauty chiefly came. The other had now achieved a unity of its own; but it was loud, and vain, and endlessly repeated; and it had little harmony, but rather a clamorous unison as of many trumpets braying upon a few notes. And it essayed to drown the other music by the violence of its voice, but it seemed that its most triumphant notes were taken by the other and woven into its own solemn pattern.
>
> In the midst of this strife, whereat the halls of Ilúvatar shook and a tremor ran out into the

silences yet unmoved, Ilúvatar arose a third time, and his face was terrible to behold. Then he raised up both his hands, and in one chord, deeper than the Abyss, higher than the Firmament, piercing as the light of the eye of Ilúvatar, the Music ceased. Then Ilúvatar spoke, and he said: 'Mighty are the Ainur, and mightiest among them is Melkor; but that he may know, and all the Ainur, that I am Ilúvatar, those things that ye have sung, I will show them forth, that ye may see what ye have done. And thou, Melkor, shalt see that no theme may be played that hath not its uttermost source in me, nor can any alter the music in my despite.

For he that attempteth this shall prove but mine instrument in the devising of things more wonderful, which he himself hath not imagined....And thou, Melkor, wilt discover all the secret thoughts of thy mind, and wilt perceive that they are but a part of the whole and tributary to its glory."[143]

The song of creation is deep and wide and beautiful, slow and blended with an immeasurable sorrow. This is the cruciform nature of reality in this age. The sorrow cannot be simply extracted from the song. No, the beauty and the sorrow are inextricably linked. This does not mean that this song is not beautiful or good because it is filled with sorrowful melodies instead of only rhythms of joy. This song of creation is good and beautiful, and God in His love for all that He has made, and in His very nature as the source of all beauty, will not allow the discordant song to ruin the symphony. In fact, He is even going to weave the notes that do not feel like they belong in the song of creation into the music in such a way that, in the final resolution of the song's completion, we will perceive that all of the attempts to dis-order the song have actually been redemptively incorporated into the perfect symphony with not a single note in all of history wasted.

We hear in Tolkien's symbolic mythology echoes of Paul's promise to the church at Rome, "We know that in all things God works for the good of those who love him, who have been called according to his purposes." God is weaving together every single note in the song of creation into a final beautiful and good composition. This does not mean that all things are presently good or beautiful or true, but it does mean that those who are pursuing the purposes of God in creation will have even the darkest instances of evil they experienced in their lives redemptively incorporated into the final harmonious and beautiful song.

As we wrestle with God through our questions about pain, suffering, loss, and evil, we need not be able to categorize every instance of order, non-order, and dis-order perfectly. It's not on you and me to save the world. We trust that He is "making all things new" (Revelation 21:5). We all see in part, and your theodicy may change throughout the years just as mine has. Hopefully, those changes even mark improvements in perspective. What we can have is confidence that God is composing the most beautiful of all possible songs, of which each of our lives plays some meaningful role, no matter how small, in bringing to its completion. May you be strengthened by His grace to resist and remedy what is dis-ordered, to bring good and right-ordering to what is not yet ordered, and to rejoice when you are called to share in Christ's sufferings.

ENDNOTES

1) Paraphrased by David Hume in David Hume, "Dialogues Concerning Natural Religion," in Baggini, *Hume on Religion*, 53.

2) At least the synoptic Gospels of Matthew, Mark, and Luke

3) 1 Corinthians 13:9-12

4) Fee, Gordon D.; Fee, Gordon D.; Stuart, Douglas; Stuart, Douglas. *How to Read the Bible for All Its Worth: Fourth Edition* (p. 72). Zondervan

5) Burns, Charlene P. E.. *Christian Understandings of Evil (p. 5)*. Fortress Press.

6) Walton, John H.; Longman III, Tremper. *How to Read Job (How to Read Series)* (loc. 139 Kindle Edition). InterVarsity Press.

7) Walton, John H.; Longman III, Tremper. *How to Read Job (How to Read Series)* (loc. 381 Kindle Edition). InterVarsity Press

8) Walton & Longmann (loc 258)

9) Walton & Longmann (loc 286)

10) Hess, Richard S.. *The Old Testament: A Historical, Theological, and Critical Introduction* (p. 410). Baker Publishing Group.

11) Walton & Longman (loc 618)

12) Walton & Longman (loc 764)

13) Walton & Longman (loc 1,326)

14) Walton & Longman (loc 1,206)

15) Burns, Charlene P. E. *Christian Understandings of Evil* (p. 14). Fortress Press.

16) "Baal Zebub". Bob Becking; Pieter W. van der Horst; Karel van der

Toorn *Dictionary of Deities and Demons in the Bible*. Eerdmans

17) 1 Thessalonians 2:18

18) Martinez, Garcia "Apocalypticism in the Dead Sea Scrolls" in Collins, *The Encyclopedia of Apocalypticism: Vol I- The Origins of Apocalypticism in Judaism & Christianity.* Continuum

19) Burns, p. 17

20) George W. E. Nickelsburg and James C. VanderKam, *1 Enoch: The Hermeneia Translation* (1–12) Minneapolis: Fortress Press, 2012.

21) James VanderKam, *Book of Jubilees (Guides to the Apocrypha and Pseudepigrapha)* (New York: Bloomsbury T&T Clark, 2001), 21–44.

22) There are some like OT Scholar, Michael Heiser who argue for acts of God's judgment on the pagan gods of Israel's polytheist neighbors being acts of judgment on demons and fallen principalities, but just by another name.

23) Stokes RE. "Not over Moses 'Dead Body: Jude 9, 22-24 and the Assumption of Moses in their Early Jewish Context." *Journal for the Study of the New Testament.* 2017;40(2):192-213.

24) Gammie, J. G. (1974). "Spatial and Ethical Dualism in Jewish Wisdom and Apocalyptic Literature." *Journal of Biblical Literature*, 93(3), 356–385.

25) This is by no means an exhaustive list of theological or philosophical contributors in the global, historic Christian tradition. To some, the selections may seem too Euro-centric and male-centric, but this is more a feature of the real historical factors of past Christian theology and philosophy than any intentional bias on my part. I am excited by the increasing opportunity for both male and female voices from diverse socio-cultural contexts to have a more prominent role in shaping Christian theology.

26) Tertullian, *The Prescription Against Heretics (chapter 36).* https://www.newadvent.org/fathers/0311.htm

27) Brent, Allen (2006). *Ignatius of Antioch and the Second Sophistic: A Study of an Early Christian Transformation of Pagan Culture.* Tübingen: Mohr Siebeck.

28) Fr. Paolo O. Pirlo, SHMI (1997). "St. Polycarp". *My First Book of Saints. Sons of Holy Mary Immaculate.* Quality Catholic Publications. pp. 58–59

29) Fr. Paolo O. Pirlo, SHMI (1997). "St. Polycarp". *My First Book of Saints. Sons of Holy Mary Immaculate.* Quality Catholic Publications. pp. 58–59

30) Burns, p. 29

31) "The Apostle of the Heretics": Paul, Valentinus, and Marcion". In Porter, Stanley E.; Yoon, David (eds.). *Paul and Gnosis. Pauline Studies. Vol. 9.* Leiden and Boston: Brill Publishers. pp. 105–118.

32) Scheidel, Walter (2006). "Growing up Fatherless in Antiquity: The Demographic Background". Princeton/Stanford Working Papers in Classics: 2.

33) Justin Martyr, "Second Apology," *Early Christian Writings*, ed. Peter.Kirby, http://www.earlychristianwritings.com/text/justinmar tyr-secondapology.html. In Burns, Charlene P. E.. *Christian Understandings of Evil* (p. 42).

34) Justin Martyr, "First Apology," Early Christian Writings, ed. Peter Kirby, http://www.earlychristianwritings.com/text/justinmartyr-firstapology.html. In Burns, Charlene P. E.. Christian Understandings of Evil (p. 42). Fortress Press

35) Irenaeus, "The Proof of the Apostolic Preaching, Chapter 12," trans. J. Armitage Robinson, D. D., *TranslationsofChristianLiterature, series IV* (New York: The Macmillan Co., 1920), 69–151. In Burns, p. 42

36) Irenaeus, *Against Heresies* (5.21.1) in A. Roberts and J. Donaldson (eds), *The Writings of Irenaeus Vol. 2* (Edinburgh: T & T Clark, 1869), p. 110-111

37) Edwards, Mark J., "Origen", *The Stanford Encyclopedia of Philosophy* (Summer 2022 Edition), Edward N. Zalta (ed.)

38) J. Wilberding. "'Creeping Spatiality': The Location of Nous in Plotinus' Universe." *Phronesis* 50, no. 4 (2005): 315–34.

39) Burns, p. 47

40) Burns,p. 49

41) Burns, p. 49

42) Plotinus *The Enneads* (4.3.12) translated by Stephen MacKenna and Eric Steinhart. http://ericsteinhart.com/resources/Enneads2015.pdf

43) *Ibid*

44) Burns, p. 50

45) Gregory of Nyssa, "The Great Catechism," 6, in *Nicene and Post-Nicene Fathers, vol. 5, second series, Gregory of Nyssa: Dogmatic Treatises*, ed. Phillip Schaff and Henry Wace (Peabody: Hendrickson, 1994).

46) *Ibid* in Burns, p. 55

47) Ibid.

48) Ibid.

49) Gregory of Nyssa, "On Virginity," 12, in *Nicene and Post-Nicene Fathers, vol. 5, second series* (Peabody: Hendrickson, 1994); in Burns, p. 56.

50) Gregory of Nyssa, "The Great Catechism," 5

51) Ibid.,29. In Burns, p. 57.

52) Ibid., 24

53) Cat. Orat. ch. 26, Migne, Tract. Filius subjicietur,--on I Cor. xv:28--pasa he anthropine phusis, "The whole of humanity." in Allin, Thomas. Parry, Robin (ed). *Christ Triumphant: Universalism Asserted as the Hope of the Gospel on the Authority of Reason, the Fathers, and Holy Scripture. Annotated Edition* . Wipf and Stock.

54) Burns, p. 58

55) Burns, p. 61

56) Burns, p. 61

57) Augustine, *On the Morals of the Manicheans.* (chapter 4). https://www.newadvent.org/fathers/1402.htm

58) Augustine, *On the Morals of The Manicheans.* (Chapter 7) https://www.newadvent.org/fathers/1402.htm

59) Augustine, *On Marriage and Concupiscence, Book II (chapter 20).* https://www.newadvent.org/fathers/15072.htm

60) Burns, p. 64

61) Augustine, *On the Morals of The Manicheans.* (Chapter 7) https://www.newadvent.org/fathers/1402.htm

62) Burns, p. 80

63) Burns, p. 80

64) Feser, Edward. 2017. *Five proofs of the existence of God.* Ignatius Press

65) Hajar R. *The Air of History (Part II) Medicine in the Middle Ages.* Heart Views. 2012. (p. 158-62).

66) https://www.nationalgeographic.com/science/article/the-plague

67) Brian Davies, Thomas Aquinas on God and Evil (New York: Oxford University Press, 2011), 92. In Burns, (p. 117).

68) Burns, 85

69) Burns, p. 85

70) Thomas Aquinas, "Question 163: The first man's sin" *Summa Theologica.* https://www.newadvent.org/summa/3163.htm#article1

71) Burns, 87

72) *Luther's Works*, American ed., 55 vols., ed. Jaroslav Pelikan and Helmut T. Lehman (Philadelphia: Muehlenberg and Fortress Press; St. Louis: Concordia, 1955–86), in Burns, p. 92.

73) Luther, as quoted in Veli-Matti Kärkkäinen, *One with God: Salvation as Deification and Justification* (Collegeville: Liturgical Press, 2004), 42.

74) Burns, 94

75) Ibid.

76) Heiko A. Oberman, Luther: Man Between God and the Devil (New York: Doubleday, 1992), 104–6

77) *Luther's Works*, p. 54

78) Burns, p. 97

79) Luther, Martin. *Commentary on Romans* (chapter 8)

80) Thomas, Matthew J. *Paul's "Works of the Law" in the Perspective of Second-Century Reception.* IVP Academic (2020)

81) John Calvin, *Institutes of the Christian Religion*, trans. Henry Beveridge (Edinburgh: The Calvin Translation Society, 1845), 2.4.5

82) Ibid., 3.21.5

83) John Wesley. "Free Grace- A Sermon Preached at Bristol" *Early English Books Online Text Creation Partnership*, 2011

84) Craig, William Lane. in Meister, C.V. (2017) *God and the Problem of Evil (Spectrum Multiview Book Series)* (p. 39). InterVarsity Press.

85) Ibid., p. 39

86) MacGregor, Kirk R. (2018). *Luis De Molina: The Life and Theology of the Founder of Middle Knowledge.*(p. 241): Zondervan

87) Carey in *God and the Problem of Evil* (p. 131)

88) Moore, A. Bollard, B. (1988) *Batman: The Killing Joke.* DC Comics.

89) Burns, p. 102

90) Schwartz, Oscar. "In the 17th Century, Leibniz Dreamed of a Machine That Could Calculate Ideas- The machine would use an "alphabet of human thoughts" and rules to combine them". *IEEE Spectrum.* (November, 2019) https://spectrum.ieee.org/in-the-17th-century-leibniz-dreamed-of-a-machine-that-could-calculate-ideas

91) Burns, p. 109

92) Burns, p. 109

93) Burns, p. 111

94) Burns, p.112

95) Look, Brandon C., "Gottfried Wilhelm Leibniz", *The Stanford Encyclopedia of Philosophy* (Spring 2020 Edition), Edward N. Zalta (ed.)

96) Voltaire, Candide (New York: Boni & Liveright , 1918), 3–4. In Burns, p. 107

97) Burns, p. 108

98) Immanuel Kant, *Prolegomena to Any Future Metaphysics*, trans. and ed. Gary Hatfield, rev. ed. (Cambridge: Cambridge University Press, 2004), 10. In Burns, p. 123

99) Gonzalez, Justo L.. *The Story of Christianity: Volume 2: The Reformation to the Present Day* (p. 259). HarperCollins.

100) Rohlf, Michael, "Immanuel Kant", *The Stanford Encyclopedia of Philosophy* (Fall 2020 Edition), Edward N. Zalta (ed.)

101) Immanuel Kant, *Lectures on Philosophical Theology*, trans. A. W. Ward and G. M. Clark (Ithaca: Cornell University Press, 1978), 125. In Burns, p. 123

102) Burns, p. 125

103) Burns, p. 129

104) Burns, p. 132

105) Ibid.

106) Friedrich Schleiermacher, *The Christian Faith*, ed. H. R. Mackintosh and J. S. Stewart (Edinburgh: T&T Clark, 1989) §80.1–4.

107) Burns, p. 126

108) Burns, 150

109) See my podcast series on *Deep Talks: Exploring Theology & Meaning-Making* entitled "Darwin, The Bible Science, & Theology"

110) Burns, 149

111) *Letter from Darwin to Asa Gray*, May 22, 1860, Darwin Correspondence Project, https://www.darwinproject.ac.uk/letter/entry-2814

112) Burns, p. 151

113) Burns, p. 152

114) Paley, William *Natural Theology: or, Evidences of the Existence and Attributes of The Deity, Collected from the Appearances of Nature* (1802), 490.

115) Friedrich Nietzsche, *The Gay Science* (1882, 1887) para. 125; Walter Kaufmann ed. (New York: Vintage, 1974), pp.181-82.

116) Burns, p. 164

117) Barmen Declaration". *Center for Barth Studies- Princeton Theological Seminary.* https://barth.ptsem.edu/major-works/

118) Johnson, K.L. (2019). Barth on Natural Theology. In The Wiley Blackwell Companion to Karl Barth (eds G. Hunsinger and K.L. Johnson).

119) Karl Barth, *Church Dogmatics, III.3*, ed. G. W. Bromiley and T. F. Torrance, trans. G. W. Bromiley and R. J. Ehrlich (Edinburgh: T&T Clark, 1960), 289.

120) Burns, p. 165

121) Barth, *Church Dogmatics, III.3*, 296–97, 302. In Burns, p.166.

122) Burns, p. 167

123) Barth, *Church Dogmatics* II.1

124) Barth. "Matthias Barth: 1 Corinthians 13:12" in Michael D. Bush;Nicholas Wolterstorff. *This Incomplete One: Words Occasioned by the Death of a Young Person* (Kindle Location 131). (2006) Eerdmans. Kindle Edition.

125) Burns, p. 173

126) David Ray Griffin, "Creation Out of Chaos and the Problem of Evil," in Davis, Encountering Evil, 105. Griffin deleted this phrase in the 2001 revision of this essay for a second edition. He did not, however, revise his stance that his theory resolves the logical problem. In Burns, p.176

127) Burns, p 177-178

128) Burns, p.177

129) Ibid.

130) Joseph A. Bracken, S.J., *Christianity and Process Thought: Spirituality for a Changing World* (West Conshohocken: Templeton, 2006), 19.

131) Burns,p. 185

132) Clark Pinnock, Richard Rice, John Sanders, William Hasker, and David Basinger, The Openness of God: A Biblical Challenge to the Traditional Understanding of God (Downers Grove, IL: InterVarsity, 1994).

133) Boyd, Greg. "On The Calvinism Debate in Chicago Last Week" (September 1, 2014) Reknew.org. https://reknew.org/2014/09/on-the-calvinism-debate-in-chicago-last-week/

134) Boyd, Gregory A. 2001. *God of the Possible: a Biblical Introduction to the Open View of God.* Grand Rapids, Mich: Baker Books

135) Boyd, Gregory A. 2007. *Satan and the Problem of Evil: Constructing a Trinitarian Warfare Theodicy.* Downers Grove, Ill: InterVarsity Press.

136) Ibid.

137) Koenig-Robert, R., Pearson, J. "Decoding the contents and strength of imagery before volitional engagement". *Sci Rep* 9, 3504 (2019).

138) *God and the Problem of Evil*, p. 56

139) See Nowak, Martin A., and Sarah Coakley. 2013. *Evolution, Games, and God: the Principle of Cooperation.* ; Nancey Murphy "Science and Society" in McClendon Jr., J.W. *Witness: Systematic Theology Vol 3.* Abindgon Press

140) Vervaeke, John. *Awakening from the Meaning Crisis*, Episode 17. https://youtu.be/mXfK4nicygA

141) David Bentley Hart, "Traditio Deformis". *First Things* (May 2015). https://www.firstthings.com/article/2015/05/traditio-deformis

142) Oord, Thomas Jay. *The Uncontrolling Love of God: An Open and Relational Account of Providence*. IVP Academic. 2015.

143) Tolkien, J. R. R., Christopher Tolkien, *The Silmarillion*.

ABOUT THE AUTHOR

Paul Anleitner Paul Anleitner (Master in Christian Thought, Bethel Seminary-St. Paul) is a writer, theologian of culture, pastor, and podcaster helping people navigate the intersection of theology with philosophy, culture, science, and all of our efforts to find meaning in the world.

Since 2018, he has hosted the popular podcast *Deep Talks: Exploring Theology & Meaning-Making* where he explores with scholars, theologians, scientists, and artists some of the most challenging and important ideas in our culture's quest for meaning.

Made in the USA
Middletown, DE
13 September 2022

10412658R00109